Chasing Understanding in the

JUNGLES OF VIETNAM

MY YEAR AS A "BLACK SCARF"

DOUGLAS BEED

Mechanicsburg, PA USA

Published by Sunbury Press, Inc.
Mechanicsburg, Pennsylvania

www.sunburypress.com

ISBN: 978-1-62006-802-1 (Trade paperback)
ISBN: 978-1-62006-803-8 (Mobipocket)

Library of Congress Control Number: 2017932382

FIRST SUNBURY PRESS EDITION: April 2017

Product of the United States of America
0 1 1 2 3 5 8 13 21 34 55

Set in Bookman Old Style
Designed by Crystal Devine
Cover by Terry Kennedy
Edited by Allyson Gard

Continue the Enlightenment!

CONTENTS

Douglas Beed in Vietnam, 1969

FOREWORD

DECEMBER 1968

Approximately 40 miles Northwest of Saigon

I had been on-line in Vietnam for less than a week, and already I understood there was only one certainty—there were many things to learn just to survive, and I wasn't learning them fast enough. I was in a three-man position on the kill zone of a night ambush on a fresh trail (one showing recent activity). One of the more experienced men in the group was awake on his 2½ hour watch, and my watch was coming up. I needed to sleep, but I just couldn't fall off.

Suddenly about ten to fifteen feet in front of me I heard a frighteningly loud sound. "RRHHHHRR, RRHHHRR, RRHHHRR . . . Fuck You, Fuck You, Fuck You!" I thought, "Holy shit, an enemy is right out in front of my position, behind the kill zone! That NVA fucker is taunting me and trying to scare me into revealing my exact position." I had never been so awake in my life. I must have gasped involuntarily because immediately I heard a very soft chuckle coming from the guy on watch right next to me! What the hell . . .!?

ACKNOWLEDGMENTS

I owe a great debt of gratitude to my inquisitive family members, especially my nieces and nephews, along with my older brother Dave (who double-dog dared me), all of whom pestered me until I reached the point that I began this work. Without that impetus I never would have started this book, which, thankfully, has turned into a life-changing experience.

This book would never have been completed if my fellow grunt and great friend Mike Humlicek had not saved me from my doubts when he read my first draft. His enthusiasm for my manuscript and his sleepless nights told me that I had indeed remembered some of it right. I'll never forget the night we shared this with his family. We both felt an indescribable feeling of relief as we validated our memories and finally talked about our story.

Also many thanks go to Drs. Peggy Barlett, Daniel Dahlquist, Thomas Connors, Jim Sweeney, Janet Sweeney and John Else who all provided much-needed opinions, questions, information and encouragement, while sharing their eagerness, which was essential in keeping me on track. I am also extremely grateful for the information and support offered by Kim Traw, friend and librarian extraordinaire.

And of course I thank my wife, Dr. Penny Beed, who has spent many hours supporting me in this endeavor, by cheering me on, asking questions, helping with development and revisions and serving as my principal editor.

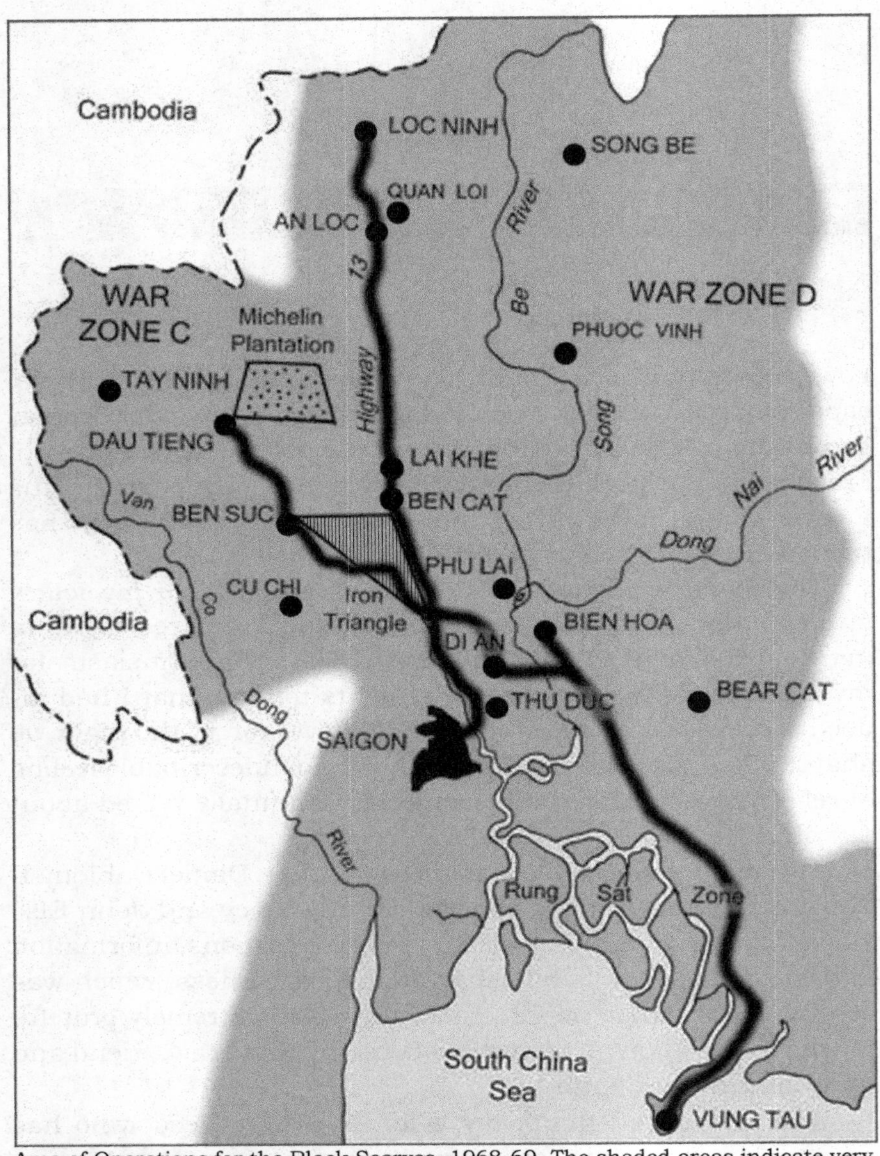

Area of Operations for the Black Scarves, 1968-69. The shaded areas indicate very heavy application of Agent Orange.

INTRODUCTION

For more than forty years, I just wanted to get on with my life and not try storing or remembering or writing or even telling many stories about my time in the army. After being back in the States from Vietnam for a couple months in 1969 and 1970, I didn't jump or twitch at loud or unexpected noises. After a year, I had bad dreams very infrequently, and after a couple of years of drinking heavily, which helped put space between me and my ghosts, I met Penny. I fell in love, got married and successfully went back and finished college. I was starting to live a life again. Things seemed to work better when I would keep the parts of my life concerning my army time and the time just after returning home pretty much separated from the rest of my life. I could occasionally tell a funny war story or two if the subject came up, and I would then seemingly return to my normal life.

Now that I have been persuaded to record my army memories by my nieces and nephews, I have realized that my approach to recovery has had a bearing on my memory of those times. In many cases, I find it difficult to recall with clarity the details of certain events, as well as the locations and timelines. The events in this account are as accurate as I can recall them, and I hope they are close enough to enable my readers to at least understand the essence of my experiences. As the lyrics of the World War II song *A Nightingale Sang in Berkeley Square* say, "I may be right; I may be wrong. But I'm perfectly willing to swear." This is the best I can do.

I would also emphasize for readers not in my generation: MY infantry was not a volunteer force; most of us were *involuntarily* placed into our predicament. By 1968, when I entered the army, many members of my generation were not supporting the

Author humping his M60 machine gun in the bush

Vietnam War and were against it. I am not fooled by General Westmoreland's (and others') post-war statements that most persons that went to Vietnam were volunteers. He classifies the entire number of men that enlisted in the military as volunteers instead of regarding the vast majority of them as men who involuntarily enlisted to escape the draft.

One of the consequences of an inequitable draft system and the army's recruiting methods was that the army infantry of which I was a part consisted almost entirely of soldiers that were drafted and who were either against the war initially or who would turn against it by the time they had been in-country (Vietnam) for a few months.

There are soldiers in the military that are what I call "Warriors." These are men and women who are drawn into life in the military and to the adrenaline rush and severe challenges of the life of combat. We should all thank them for their courage and for their service and sacrifices to our country. However, this book is not an account of a warrior; rather, it is an account of one of many young men ordered by their government to disrupt their plans and dreams and instead, serve their country. We who ended up in the infantry were all required to learn the skills of war-making and to perform acts of war. We too served and sacrificed but most of us did not have the motivation of a warrior. Pride of service turned out to be a very different notion for us than it is today with an all-voluntary force. I believe our experiences were akin to the drafted combat soldiers throughout our country's long military history.

So as you begin reading my account, keep in mind that we involuntary draftees in Mike Platoon for the most part learned and performed our jobs well. We all endured frequent short firefights that were in line with our mission. Most of them all blend into one morphed memory of us doing our job well and efficiently. When I am asked, "What did you do in the war?" these are the stories that creep into my mind. Have at it.

PART 1

STATESIDE

"May you be cursed to live in interesting times."
—Daniel Dahlquist
(Adapted from *The Chinese Curse*)

CHAPTER 1

JOINING THE CLUB

11 Months earlier—January 1968, Cedar Rapids, IA

My story began in January 1968 as I was just finishing my first two years of college at Ellsworth Junior College in Iowa Falls, IA. My father had died when I was a junior in high school, and I had no money and no idea of what I wanted to do with my life. I had had a great liberal arts experience during the past two years. I had studied some things that didn't interest me; I had also discovered several exciting subjects that I might like to pursue. The difficulty with that academic situation was that the local Selective Service Board would draft a man if he didn't successfully complete thirty credit hours in a specific degree program each academic year. I would have liked to experiment with a couple of interesting majors, but I didn't have the money, and it was apparent that the Selective Service wouldn't allow me the time to explore. Besides, all of the four-year schools that I would have attended next were much more expensive, so I didn't transfer. Instead, I let my student deferment lapse on January 31, 1968.

Two days later, on February 2, I received a notice in my mailbox to report in ten days for my pre-induction medical examination at Fort Des Moines. The local county draft board had processed my change of status from 2S (student deferment) to 1A (draft-eligible) and had mailed the notice, all in the span of one eight-hour day. Wow! I have always felt that many other federal agencies could learn a few things about efficiency of operations if they would take the time and energy to study the Linn County Selective Service Board's organization in the early months of 1968. I can tell you with unconditional conviction that the US Army never came close to that level of competence. The door into what we later would call the "great green meat grinder" was now wide open for me to enter.

Simultaneously, some very important geopolitical events were unfolding for the United States. January 31, 1968 was the beginning of the 1968 Tet Offensive in Vietnam. The first week of February 1968 is considered by many historians as the most important week in the Vietnam War; the North Vietnam Army (NVA) and the Viet Cong (VC) successfully surprised and set on its heels the combined armies of the US, South Vietnam and their other allies. The Tet Offensive was a stunning reversal to the "light at the end of the tunnel" assessment that the US Generals and politicians were promoting to our country. During the month of February, 1968 the US military had an average of 513 men killed and 2500+ wounded each week; these turned out to be the heaviest weekly casualties of the war.

The allied forces eventually won a complete victory over the NVA and VC forces committed to this massive offensive action. During this campaign, we sustained an unusually high casualty rate for us, but their losses were catastrophic for them. It is reported that many of their units suffered 90% casualty rates, and therefore the North was not able to have another offensive action for over two years. Even with these outcomes, the damage to the American public's trust of their government and military was shattered.

Back at home, all of the military branches were stunned. Few people remember, but in the spring of 1968, the Army, the Navy and the Marines were all frantically drafting men. It was a very frightening time for the US military and for the men that were forced into the system at that time. It was into this military panic that I entered the military draft machine.

When I reported to Fort Des Moines in February for my pre-induction physical, I entered an unnerving, confusing system designated to find an increasing number of new and replacement bodies for the military quickly. For me personally, it was an astonishing world of life-threatening choices. Each branch was grabbing replacements for their huge losses of the weeks before. The "great green meat grinder" was grabbing live bodies at a frenzied pace.

I now think I overreacted but, instead of passively letting them draft me, I asked to meet with an US Army recruiter. I simply asked him what enlistment programs with a two-year contract he had available. I didn't want to enlist for more than the two years that a drafted man would spend in the military. He told me that he had a two year OCS program (Officer Candidate – 2nd Lieutenant School) or a two-year WOC (Warrant Officer Candidate School – helicopter pilot school) program. In both cases, you would finish a one-year training program and then sign a new multiyear contract with the army. I didn't want to be an officer, so I enlisted in the WOC program. Go Army—Go WOC!

I reported back to Fort Des Moines in mid-April and took my oath to serve diligently and faithfully in the US Army. During this time, most men drafted from Eastern Iowa were sent to Fort Leonard Wood in Missouri for their Basic Training. But since I had actually enlisted into US Army Flight School I was sent unaccompanied to Fort Polk, Louisiana.

CHAPTER 2

FORT POLK

The only memory of my trip to Fort Polk is that I flew through Dallas where my high school friend Jane Cherry met me in Love Field during my late night layover. She was a student at Southern Methodist University and drove to the airport to have a short visit and see me off. It was a very nice act of kindness that I have never forgotten. It was perfectly timed. Thank you, Jane. I now realize that her visit with me was the last remnant of my former life. From here on out a huge change was about to engulf me and I would never be the same.

I then boarded the plane and, after a delay due to an engine problem, we took off two or three hours late for Fort Polk, Louisiana. What a ride! Through the years I have forgotten a number of fire fights that I was in, but I have never forgotten the

DC3 (Courtesy www.flickr.com)

New Military ID made on 2nd or 3rd day of Basic Training

details of that first flight into Hell. The DC3 couldn't or didn't fly around or over that huge mid-April thunder storm; it flew through it. I remember a flight attendant who was strapped in and seriously not confident, blinking cabin and warning lights, severe drops in altitude, the startled whites of the flight attendant's eyes and the twisting and turning of the cabin during that long flight.

Boy, was I glad to get out of the plane and stand on the soil of Fort Polk! What a fool I was. I soon found that Fort Polk was a hellhole.

We all departed the plane and waited until a semi-trailer truck pulling a flatbed trailer with rudimentary sides and benches on the trailer bed pulled up for us. We climbed aboard and were delivered to a large asphalt pad some time past midnight. It is now difficult to recall the size of the lot, but I do remember hundreds of four-inch dots painted in rows and columns six feet apart on the asphalt pad. Each of us was directed to stand on one of those dots until our name was called. Through the night I would guess that the population of that pad would dwindle down to 150 to 200 people and, as a new wave of men would arrive, it would increase to 500 to 600. I stood on my four-inch dot until around 5:00 a.m. when someone called my name and I entered a building to begin processing. I had been in the army for less than 24 hours, but already I knew for certain that my life was no longer mine.

In this basic training photo I am standing on the right.

Within another 24 hours we were all dressed alike, groomed alike and stripped of our former identities alike. I reported to Company B, 1st Battalion, 1st Basic Training Brigade on the edge of Ft. Polk, LA. We had one barbed wire fence between us and civilian life, and for the next eight weeks that soil on the other side of the fence taunted us.

We were now living in a World War I barracks with not a single partition in the bunk area or in the latrine area. There were thirty-some men on each floor to share these accommodations, and we had absolutely no privacy anywhere. The only break we had was an occasional short religious ceremony in the company area on Sundays.

One weekend, if we qualified on our M14 weapons, we were allowed to leave post on Friday night and report back late Saturday afternoon. I literally got on a bus, went to Lake Charles (as far away as I could get), rented a motel room, fell asleep immediately, woke up in the morning, bought breakfast and took the bus back to Fort Polk. Being away and alone was a great morale booster for me.

For eight weeks, we slowly learned the fundamentals of being a soldier. We learned in classrooms, in labs, on ranges, on our knees and on our bellies. We probably learned something in our sleep or at least when we should have been asleep. I just don't remember much except for flashes of the numerous times we arrived back at the barracks late at night, so exhausted, dirty and wet that we actually just walked into the shower and hosed off our bodies, our clothes and even our weapons to begin cleaning up. Needless to say, we were soon without hot water.

Basic Training was dreadful. It seemed an eternity and it tested us to our limits, but there was no choice other than to progress further on their continuum or be sent back a cycle and spend more time in hell. Week by week we marched forward, and by the time we graduated we were part of the "Green Machine." Anyone who didn't graduate was in a Federal Prison, doing long-term Brig time, in a Psycho facility or on the run. I was then ordered to Fort Wolters, Texas, where I would begin my helicopter flight schooling.

CHAPTER 3

FORT WOLTERS

I arrived in Texas, and my personal hell continued. The first four weeks of "Flight Training" involved Pre-Flight Training, which was designed to "wash out" the solders that really didn't want to be pilots. Consequently, every moment was designed to be as difficult as possible. There were high academic standards, high physical requirements and high bullshit requirements. This phase of training consisted of just another stepped-up, exhausting routine. I was meeting all of the requirements, but during my three weeks in pre-flight training I learned that, because of the secret security clearance and the high test scores needed to qualify as a WOC, the WOC program dropouts were getting jobs as clerk typists at the Pentagon. Since that was really my goal, I quit the US Army Flight Training program and was assigned to the "Casual Company."

The Casual Company was a group of men who were awaiting orders for their new assignments in the army. It usually took two to three weeks for new orders to arrive for the individual soldier. During this time, there were very few jobs for these soldiers, except every week or two we would be assigned to help pick up helicopter and body parts if a student pilot crashed. As I remember, I was fortunate and never actually had to respond to a crash during this casual time.

Labor Day weekend occurred during my casual time at Fort Wolters. Hoping a helicopter crash wouldn't occur and knowing that there were no staff members to check on our whereabouts, I decided to go AWOL (Absent without Leave) and return to Iowa for the long weekend. So without a pass I took a bus into Dallas, jumped on a plane to Chicago and then Cedar Rapids and hitchhiked up to Delhi, IA. I had a fun weekend swimming and relaxing with family and friends and got back to Fort Wolters by midnight Monday. No one had noticed.

Bad news came soon! At approximately the same time I had found out about the "Pentagon Clerk Express" and dropped out of the flight training, the army had decided that too many soldiers were dropping out of WOC training and that the situation needed to stop immediately. As a result, since my name started with the letter B, I was the first person listed on the first set of orders to end the dropout problem. From these orders on, all WOC dropouts were to be trained as infantry soldiers and condemned to the infantry. My orders directed me to report to Fort Lewis, Washington for Advanced Infantry Training (AIT).

CHAPTER 4

FORT LEWIS

The most vivid memory I have of Fort Lewis is of the absolutely beautiful setting. The evergreen forests and mountains that surrounded us were breathtaking to a kid that grew up in the Midwest. From almost anywhere on the post, if it was a clear day, we could see beautiful Mount Rainier. After a while all of us in infantry training were starting to develop our trademark pessimistic humor; we referred to Mount Rainier as Mount Rain-Gear since it rained so much in the Seattle area. The infantry view of life was this: if you couldn't see Mt. Rain-Gear, it was raining; if you could see it, it was *going to* rain.

I reported to the First Sergeant at Company B, 1st Battalion, 3rd Brigade for my Advanced Infantry Training (AIT). Just as in Fort Polk and Fort Wolters, I was housed in World War 1 barracks. Of course these were the only World War 1 barracks on the entire post and the infantry trainees got the honor of living in them. I was never assigned to any sleeping structure in the states that was built after World War 1 or that had any interior walls. The honor and pride that the US Army has for its infantry were never extended to me.

Infantry training was hard work. We spent weeks learning about different weapons; we spent more weeks on the firing ranges learning proficiency with those weapons, and then we spent even more weeks of learning and practicing infantry tactics at the squad, platoon and company levels. Physical training was a large part of every day. They would load us down with every heavy object they could find and make us run somewhere.

We ran five miles before breakfast. We ran to every class. We would run the obstacle course multiple times every week. Later we would crawl through the live fire course several times. We were always running, jumping, crawling or climbing, while carrying lots of weight. Then to rest we would run over to the clinic to get more shots and do the 50 required post-shot pushups. We were exhausted.

All of this loaded-down running did have a purpose though; it was a peek into the future. Later, flying into an LZ (landing zone) in Vietnam, loaded down with our "Basic Combat Load," we would jump off and run away from the helicopter towards the tree or brush line in much better shape than if we had not trained in this way.

One of the men in our training platoon at Fort Lewis was 39 years old and had enlisted to become an army firefighter. He had been in the military before and then became a civilian firefighter. Now he wanted to get back into the service as a firefighter. Somehow the army had his training assignment mixed up and had sent him to Fort Lewis and into infantry training. At his age, he could hardly make it through each of these rigorous days. Even though he was in a wrong assignment, he didn't want to fail in this training because he knew that it would be bad for him to have any failure in his record. So he kept hanging in and tried to finish each day.

Finally his adjusted orders arrived and he was ordered to the correct army schooling. That night he and two squads of his friends sneaked out of the barracks, went to the Enlisted Men's Club to celebrate his leaving, and got drunk on whiskey and beer boilermakers. The next day was a full training day, and all we did was puke and drink water all day.

The time at Fort Lewis was a very difficult time for me. The physical training was a challenge, but the more difficult part was adjusting to the reality of going into the real war in a role that was very intimidating. Very few people wanted to do what I was in the midst of training to do. All through my different stations in the army I kept hoping that I would end up anywhere but where I was now. That's what we all thought about in our quiet moments.

As the weeks ticked by, in spite of our dread, we all clung to the slight hope that we would somehow receive orders to report to Germany or Korea. Most of our hopes evaporated during the sixth or seventh week when we reported to the quartermaster to be issued new uniforms. Even though it was a well-guarded secret about which of us were to report to Vietnam, only two lucky soldiers in our company were issued white underwear and shirts for being stationed in Germany or Korea; the rest of us were issued green ones. From that moment on, we knew our fates were sealed.

The last week of training was bivouac week, which is a large five day-and-night lab in which all of our training was put to a personal test. I remember taking my three-hour watch while my other two companions slept. We were supposed to be battle ready in our foxhole during our watch time. The problem was that the 3½ foot deep foxhole had two feet of frigid water in it. As I was lying down beside my foxhole, trying to keep dry, I heard our sergeant walking his rounds to check on us. So I quietly lowered myself into the two feet of water, letting him walk by. As a result, I was doomed to be cold and wet for the next 12 or more hours.

The climax of bivouac week was going through the Night Infiltration Course. This was an exercise in which a soldier had to use map reading, compass and navigation skills as well as the skill of moving through the forest quietly. We had eight hours to navigate five or six kilometers (clicks) without being caught by the "enemy," who were our training and other support staff. I remember that three or four of us got together to plan our strategy. On our map, we noticed that about ½ kilometer (about .3 mile) outside the side of the course boundary was a country road. So we set up our strategy, which was to go forward about ¾ of a kilometer, take a hard right and get on the other side of the county road and out of the Infiltration Course and all of its inherent dangers. We would then quietly walk down five clicks, out of sight, while keeping the road just in our view. Then we would very slowly and quietly cross over the road back into the infiltration course and cross the finish line. So that's what we did: we first got to the other side of the road (outside of the course) rather quickly. We then walked the five clicks towards the finish area. After we finished the five clicks, we patiently watched the road and the other side for a very long time. We knew that if there was anything worse than being caught by the staff in the course it was being caught by the staff outside the course. When we ascertained there was no activity over there, we slowly crossed the road back into the Infiltration Course. Then again we watched the area ahead of us for another extended time. Finally, we confirmed that we had pulled it off. We quietly and innocently walked toward the campfires and were congratulated by some of the staff for doing a great job. Quite frankly, it was a great job.

Somehow the bad dream of Advanced Infantry Training finally ended. I was given a ten-day leave, along with orders to report to Oakland, California for shipment to Vietnam.

CHAPTER 5

PROCESSING OUT AND LEAVING THE STATES

I had a hell of a time getting home to Iowa. It was late November, and I had to fly military standby on each of four legs from Seattle to Omaha. On the flight from Boise to Denver, I actually flew on one of the jump seats used by the crew. The plane was full, but the crew knew there was a seat available on my Denver flight. I think that they simply didn't want to leave me stranded overnight in Boise, so they put me on a jump seat. I now wonder if my name was even on their manifest. The airline crews were always respectful to us, but there were few acts of kindness by the public for us soldiers in 1968.

I remember getting into Omaha late at night and being met by my mom, my brother Don, my sister Bev and my good friend Jim Ibeling. We had a long ride to Cedar Rapids and got home at around four or five in the morning. I don't remember any of us taking a nap. I think we just talked all the way home. I remember spending time with family and visiting friends and then suddenly my ten days were finished. I don't even remember the farewell that probably took place for my departure. I'm sure by that time my mind was somewhere else.

The next memory I have is of a World War I-era wooden building called "the barn" that was located in the Oakland, California, Processing Center. The open interior of the barn seemed to be somewhere between one and two square blocks in area. It had bunk beds four high and the lights were blazing 24 hours a day. As I was processed, my name would be called and I would leave the barn for an auxiliary building to complete some processing and would then be sent back to the barn until my name was called again. We fell asleep between tasks and listened for our names in our sleep.

PART 2

SETTLING INTO NAM

CHAPTER 6

PROCESSING IN NAM

At some point on December 4, 1968 my name was called, and my duffel bag and I were loaded onto a bus and taken to Travis Air Force base. We all climbed aboard a chartered United Air Lines stretch DC9. As I recall, the flight over was a very quiet time, but then it could have been rowdy because I'm not sure I would have known. I think I was simply buried in my own thoughts. The flight crew was very nice and respectful but pretty much just left us alone. We stopped in Hawaii to refuel and did the same on Wake Island. I remember approaching tiny Wake Island and thinking there was no way this aircraft could land on that airstrip. I will say that the plane braked at a rate at least twice the rate I have ever experienced since. I think that the next refueling stop was Okinawa, Japan. We then flew into Tan Son Nhut Air Force Base near Saigon in Vietnam. The date of our arrival was December 5, 1968.

As we came in on our approach to Tan Son Nhut, I remember being struck by the utter beauty of the landscape, something I had never expected. I remember lush green forests with rivers winding through the green. It was breathtakingly beautiful. When we disembarked, we were hit by hot humid air that smelled of diesel fuel and canvas. To this day whenever I smell diesel fuel or damp canvas, I am immediately transported back to Vietnam or Fort Polk. When we were walking across the tarmac towards the terminal I remember so clearly a file of men walking towards another aircraft. These men were going home. I wondered whether I would ever have that experience, and, if I did, what my thoughts would be. I could not fathom what their thoughts were as I watched them with so much envy.

Somehow or another I got onto another bus and was transported up the road to the 90th Replacement Battalion, located in a huge army base called Bien Hoa. One odd part of the 90th that I noticed was a huge fenced-in area that I would estimate to be 50 feet by 80 feet in size or maybe even larger. It was filled with all of the jungle fatigues turned in by the men that were leaving Vietnam. Little did I know that these discarded uniforms very soon would be part of my life.

It was here at the 90th that my hopes for a safer assignment were rekindled. Bien Hoa was one of the biggest and safest army facilities in the country. During our two days of processing I saw a few young men that must have been assigned to infantry units that were stationed in and around Bien Hoa. My guess was that their units were in charge of the security of areas around the base. I memorized the units that they were assigned to and I hoped that my assignment would be one of those units. No such luck. I was directed to report to Alpha Company, First of the Second Infantry Battalion, First Infantry Division at Lai Khe. I was issued four new sets of jungle fatigues with my name and the First Infantry Division patches on and was trucked to the airstrip for a flight to Lai Khe.

CHAPTER 7

WELCOME TO THE FIRST OF THE SECOND INFANTRY BATTALION

My battalion, the First of the Second Infantry Battalion, was an old and proud unit and the lifers (career military personnel) loved being a part of it. There were two battalions of the 2nd Regiment: the 1st of the 2nd and the 2nd of the 2nd (written as 1/2 and 2/2 Infantry battalions). The original 2nd Infantry Regiment was formed in March 1791 and has been active ever since. In Vietnam the 1st battalion was known as the "Black Scarves Battalion" because each soldier wore a black silk scarf made from a large quantity of silk captured from the Viet Cong after a large battle early in the war. The Viet Cong and North Vietnamese Army (NVA) had used this fabric to make their "Black Pajama" uniforms. We were the only infantry unit authorized to wear a scarf as part of our uniforms. The infantry crossed rifle symbol was embroidered on each scarf with a company letter placed in the upper quadrant and the battalion number designation in the bottom quadrant. The entire ½ symbol was stitched in a different color for each company: Company A was in red, Company B was in white, Company C was in blue, Company D was in green and Headquarters Company was in yellow.

The lifers loved the history, the tradition, and the distinction of being in the First of the Second Battalion. They became a part

The ever-present Black Scarf

of an old and storied institution and most were inspired and determined to be bold and remarkable leaders. To us grunts in the field it was just another symbol of the burden of the lifers' expectations.

To help the reader, here is some basic information about 1st Division Infantry unit sizes. In 1968, the makeup of the combat units in my division was as follows (in order from smallest to largest unit):

Unit Term and Number of Men	Number of Units
Squad, four to six men or two three-man machine gun crews	4 squads per platoon: 1 point squad, 2 rifle squads, 1 machine gun squad
Platoon, sixteen to twenty five men	4 platoons per company: 3 rifle platoons, 1 mortars platoon
Company, (Co), ninety to one hundred and ten men	5 Companies per battalion: A, B, C, D (in the field), HHC (headquarters in basecamp)
Battalion, (Bn), 750 to 1,500 men	5 Bn in our brigade
Brigade, (Bde), 3,000 to 5,000	3 Bde per division: 1st, 2nd, 3rd

Unit Term and Number of Men	Number of Units
Regiment	Military unit consisting usually of a number of battalions, in my case 2 (1/2 Inf and 2/2 Mech Inf). Historically, the regiment was the main local unit that a person was enlisted in and that the soldier identified with; however in Vietnam, there was no administrative function for the regiment since the battalions reported directly to the brigades.
1st Infantry Division, twelve to fifteen thousand men	9 Inf Battalions (Bns), 5 Artillery Bns, approximately 2 Aviation Bns, several Cavalry units, several reconnaissance units, 1 Bn each of Engineering, Medical, Supply and Transportation, Signal, Maintenance and other support units.

CHAPTER 8

GETTING TO MY COMPANY

My transportation to Lai Khe was on a C-7 Caribou troop/cargo plane. These rough and tough short-takeoff planes were used as taxis for shuttling individual troops between bases in-country (in the country of Vietnam). Evidently they were durable and reliable, but I never spent time flying in one without feeling anxious or outright scared. By my second or third flight in one, someone had given me the secret to keeping my fears somewhat in check. I was told to just watch the crew chief, and if he was filling out his paper work for the flight, the plane was not about to crash. The crew chief was an Air Force enlisted man and the last man to walk onto the plane. He would sit in the back of the fuselage and fill out military forms the entire flight. I have been in three or four helicopters in which I felt bullets hitting the body. I was even in one that was shot down; I wasn't aware of it until we landed in the Landing Zone (LZ) and the two pilots and two door gunners jumped out of the chopper with us. But without question the most scared I ever was in the air was two or three moments while flying in those damned Caribous.

There were three other men reporting to A½ Infantry with me: Jim Gray from Washta, Iowa; Mike Humlicek from Carroll, Iowa; and Rich Lovejoy from Minneapolis, Minnesota. All four of us landed in Vietnam on the same day, reported to our company on the same day and were all assigned to Mike Platoon. These three men were to become my best friends in the army. Since

C-7 Caribou (Courtesy commons.wikipedia.org.)

we all came over to Vietnam on the same date, we all shared the most important binding element of friendship that we could have; we all dreamed of flying home on the same day one year later: December 4, 1969. In addition, since we were all in the same platoon (20-25 men), every day we shared a common fate.

Lai Khe was a settlement of French colonial rubber plantation mansions. The army had built an airstrip near this settlement; then they fenced it all in, making a basecamp about 1 mile by ½ mile in size. All of the area around this French settlement consisted of miles of rubber tree plots. So except for the air strip, my memory of the Lai Khe base is of solid shade from these trees, scattered old mansions, wooden army buildings like mess halls and storage sheds, and lots of old tents of all sizes with bunkers (covered trenches for protection from enemy rocket and mortar fire) beside them. It was a very surreal landscape for an anxious wide-eyed newbie going to war. It was at once a nostalgic art deco dreamscape and a primitive town made for war.

CHAPTER 9

GETTING TO AND WORKING OUT OF DI AN

The four of us reported into A Company headquarters and were greeted by our company clerk. He was a three-year infantry volunteer who had the scars of three AK bullets passing through his chest from his first tour. We soon found out that he was a special clerk. These wounds were bad enough that his Army job was permanently changed from infantry to company clerk. This meant that he could not be sent back out in the field and that he knew all about the conditions of the grunts out there. He hated the army and army lifers. This combination made him our best friend because he devoted his time in Nam to helping the grunts in his company and screwing every lifer that he could. There were many times when he would secretly perform paper work in spite of the officers or First Sergeant and get a soldier out of the field a day early or would keep him in the rear a day or two later than otherwise would have been the case. He did everything he could to make our lives better even if it was for just one or two fewer days in the field during the year.

He issued each of us a rucksack (a backpack frame with a bag attached to it) in which we were to keep our personal belongings in the rear, but we would soon find out that things were always being stolen from them. The only possessions that were ours for a year were the things that we could keep in our pockets or in our helmet liner between our heads and the helmet; nothing else would survive. For a year, we had no permanent place to store anything.

We then turned in all of the new jungle fatigues that we had been issued three days prior at the 90th; we never saw them again. For the next twelve months, all of the clothing we were issued was trucked in from the large fenced-in area at the 90th Replacement Battalion. The clothes had anybody's identity but our own; not once were we given a replacement uniform that had any of our own information on it.

After doing a few more things with the clerk, I think we met the XO (Executive Officer-2nd in command) and then we were issued our M16 weapons, the mainstay rifle for the infantry in Vietnam. We were now ready for the field. At that time our company was patrolling around a base near the village of Di An (pronounced Zee-on). We left Lai Khe and then flew to Di An in a God Damned C-7 Caribou. The four of us who arrived together from the 90th Replacement Battalion (Gray, Humlicek, Lovejoy and myself) flew to the forward headquarters of A Company at Di An and reported to First Sergeant Wingate.

First Sergeant (or Top, slang for 1st Sergeant) Wingate was the best First Sergeant that we had during my year in Nam. He was straight and competent and he cared for his troops. I remember when he met us, he asked where we were from, and when we answered that we were from Iowa and Minnesota, he replied that we would all make fine soldiers and that he would never have to worry about our performance in the field.

Di An was a lucky and safe assignment for the company. I don't remember a single casualty during the two to three weeks that we were there. For me it was an extended safe time to get acclimated to working with my platoon and for getting into shape. That was helpful because soon, when we went up to Lai Khe and things got a lot dicier, I had a much better understanding of the platoon's soldiers and their roles in a firefight.

I only remember a couple of the patrols in which I participated when we were working out of Di An. One was on Christmas Day, 1968. We swept through a small village looking for hidden weapons. For several nights, some scattered small arms fire had been coming from the village. As we were performing our hooch-to-hooch-search (a hooch is a native built hut) several armored personnel carriers (APCs) came into the village, and suddenly I noticed that some hooches were on fire. Later I become aware that the APCs were Zippos. These were APCs with mounted flame throwers and they were burning either parts of or the entire village. There were scores of villagers crying and on their knees begging us to stop the destruction. We then wrapped up the operation and returned to Di An for a great Christmas feast! The irony of these events occurring on that Christmas Day still haunts me.

Then a week later we were on a night action because "intelligence" told our commanders that a well-respected North Vietnam Army (NVA) Battalion was going to move through our Area of Operations (AO) for the next several nights on their way to the Saigon area. So our company was ordered to set up platoon-sized ambushes on major trails to stop them from moving through the area. Oh, boy, where do I start to discuss the stupidity of that entire event? First, I was new in the country and scared shitless at the mental image of having my 25-man platoon trying to stop a battalion of 300-400 soldiers in the middle of the night. Obviously the NVA were not going to be moving in large groups because then they could very easily be found and dispatched by our air power, but I was too new to think that through. Second, how on earth did the lifer commanders think that three platoons of 25 men each from A Company could have an impact on a battalion of NVA soldiers by setting up only three ambushes, even if they moved in small groups? Wouldn't splitting into smaller groups, monitoring the trails and reporting movement be better? Finally, why did our commanders believe their local "intelligence" about large troop movements? I soon learned that at the macro level military intelligence served an important purpose and was often accurate, but at my local level little credence should have been given to it.

Late that night we were set up for an ambush in an open area with no cover, and all of a sudden, out in front of us, a US basecamp about one or two miles away started shooting flares, star clusters and small arms fire up into the air like crazy. Suddenly another US compound a few miles away in a slightly different direction started doing the same thing. Then quickly a third and a fourth light show started. We were all just about dead with panic because we initially thought that this phantom NVA Battalion had staged timed assaults on all of these US outposts and would soon be running down our trails when they broke contact with the outposts. All of those outposts had bunkers (fortified partially-underground fighting positions), concertina wire (multiple rolls of razor-sharp barbed wire), artillery and many more people and all we had were 25 men lying flat on the ground with no defenses. Then somebody noticed it was midnight on New Year's Eve. Boy, was I scared that night!

* * *

I remember getting a letter from my mom in the field one day that told me that my sister Barb, who is three years younger than I, had been in a car accident in Iowa City. Mom said that she was OK but that she had more than 200 stitches in her head and face. My mother has the most positive attitude of anyone I ever knew, so I had absolutely no idea of the shape that my sister really was in. The letter was 10 or so days old, and I had to wait another week or ten days before we went back to the basecamp. So I was very worried about Barb while waiting to get in and make a call home.

We finally got in to basecamp. As required, we all first got field-ready before doing anything else. Then I went to see Top Wingate to see if I could call home to find out about Barb. He told me to come back at 2000 hours (8:00 p.m.) and he would call the base Como (communications unit) to see if they had their Ham Radio up and running that night. To make a phone call to the states from our basecamps, a "ham" operator in camp would make contact with a "ham" operator in the states somewhere or anywhere, and then the stateside operator would call collect to the telephone number of the state-side party. Then the two operators would relay the two sides of the conversations back and forth.

I reported back to Top at 8:00 p.m., and he called over to Como to check on the possibility of making a call. He was told that they would not make connections until after 0200 hours (2:00 a.m.) and that it could take up to two hours to complete the call. These calls were made at night from Vietnam because they had to be made during the day in the states for the best results of making contact with a ham operator. Top told me that I couldn't do it because the Old Man (company CO) expected us to be awake, already fed and on the tarmac by 0430 to catch our choppers for our next insertion—end of discussion.

Of course I never did get to call home, but I finally did feel better several months later when I received a letter from my great friend George McClain who wrote that Barb would indeed be fine. Although I had received several other letters from my family, his was the first letter that I could absolutely trust to tell me the full and straight truth; thank you, George.

Well, I had a few more days and nights in the field, learned a little more about the ways of the war, and suddenly our company finished up our time in Di An. Early one morning Alpha Company walked out to the airstrip, divided into platoons and each platoon loaded into a "Shithook" (Chinook helicopter) to fly to Lai Khe. We were going back to our Battalion's main area of operation. Life was going to get a lot more hairy and we were sad to say goodbye to safe little Di An.

PART 3

GETTING DOWN TO BUSINESS

CHAPTER 10

MY MISSION AND WHERE I WORKED

The First Infantry Division was the first division created by the US Army (as the "First Expeditionary Force" in WWI) and has always been the first infantry division committed to every war since. It is a division characterized by tough army pride; its motto is "No Mission Too Difficult. No Sacrifice Too Great. Duty First." By the time I joined the fun, the division's AO (Area of Operation) was northwest of Saigon all the way to Cambodia. The mission for the Division was to prohibit movement of material and personnel of the NVA on the main infiltration routes to Saigon and South Central Vietnam. This AO was one of the most consistently active and difficult AOs in-country. My Brigade's AO (the northernmost area of the division's) included the village of Lai Khe. Lai Khe was located approximately 40 kilometers north of Saigon on Highway 13, nicknamed Thunder Road. It was the southernmost basecamp (except for the short time in Di An) that I worked out of. Our operations from Lai Khe mostly took us west into some very famous real estate: the Iron Triangle, the Trapezoid and the Ho Bo Woods. The Cambodian border was due west a few kilometers from these areas and the enemy was very busy moving and storing men and materials here. When we would go into any of those areas we would often bump into some very serious company.

Fifty kilometers north of Lai Khe is An Loc. (See map.) Twenty-two kilometers north of An Loc is Loc Ninh, which is 17 clicks (kilometers) from the Cambodian border. Loc Ninh was the North Vietnam government's Provisional Capital for "their" territory of South Vietnam. The two villages of An Loc and Loc Ninh were considered by them to be NVA territory, and there were many pitched battles in this area since they believed they were protecting their own territory. The basecamp that I worked out of the most in this area was Quan Loi, which is just outside of An Loc and a just a few clicks from Loc Ninh. Quan Loi was my Brigade's headquarters at the time. The terrain around this basecamp was mostly thick jungle or rubber farms.

At other times, we worked out of the small outpost of Song Be. Song Be was about 45 clicks east of Quan Loi and also very close to the Cambodian border. This outpost was used to support operations of finding and ambushing enemy on trails that were east of Highway 13. Song Be was very active, but what made operation there distinctive for us was the terrain and environment. It was sometimes hilly and a bit more open. It was scrub land in some places and light to heavy bamboo forests in other places.

A study of the map will reveal that we were seldom based more than 30 miles from the Cambodian border and in the

Me, Bill Gentry and Lonnie Gaston catching a breather in one of the basecamps.

middle of the many branches of the Ho Chi Minh Trail that took men and material to their war in the Saigon region. The 1st Division's Mission was not territory or key terrain or to win popular local support. The mission was centered on body count. We were in an area to find and then kill people. Everything we did 24 hours a day, every day of the year, was to locate an indication of troop movement and then to stalk and kill those people. Translated to my personal world in A ½ Infantry, it meant that I would wander through the countryside with a group of 20-25 men (platoon) looking for signs of the NVA in an area chosen to be the most likely for us to make contact with them. Then we would set up an ambush every night on the most traveled trail that we had discovered that day. Our daily life was to search for and then destroy the enemy every hour of every day.

CHAPTER 11

AMBUSH

An ambush is an offensive tactic that requires a unit, in our case a platoon of 20 to 25 men, to move to a path or trail exactly at darkness and set up a six- to eight-position kill formation (with three men in each position), designed to surprise and kill an enemy party moving on that trail. A trail or path could be an obvious track or a footpath that was unrecognizable to all except the point men. One three-man position would face to the rear and the position in the center of the formation was the Command Post (CP). The rest of the three man positions were along the kill zone. The two positions on the front corners guarded each flank and also fired on the kill zone on the trail. These corner positions contained an M60 machine gun crew. The other two or three positions between the M60 machine guns would each be manned with three men armed with M16s or M79 grenade launchers. Each position was manned by soldiers with their personal weapons. Every soldier carried an M18 A1 Claymore mine which would be placed out in front of us on the kill zone.

The Claymore mine is a soldier-detonated anti-personnel mine that is set up and aimed in a specific direction (usually the kill zone) and, when fired, shoots a pattern of steel balls like a shotgun. The scheme of the ambush was for an enemy party to walk on the trail into the kill zone, and then we would start or "pop" the ambush. This meant that all men on the kill zone would fire their Claymores and then saturate the Kill Zone with small arms fire resulting in the extermination of everyone in the zone. That sounds great, but at times things weren't that clean.

Claymore Mine with 50 feet of cord and a firing device
(Courtesy en.wikipedia.org.)

Sometimes not everyone was killed and a small fire fight would ensue; sometimes the victims would be scouts for a larger element and the rest of the larger party would run to join the fight since they now knew our exact location. Both of these outcomes were not ideal from our non-defensive positions.

When we were on ambush we were always jumpy or twitchy, listening for the sounds of the enemy. We could seldom see anything so we would interpret our world through our ears as we listened to the sounds of the night.

On an ambush one night, I began to hear the distinct sounds of a person crawling on the jungle floor directly towards our position. Instantly the other two men in my position were awake and securing something to kill the intruder silently without revealing our exact position.

The enemy may have been aware that we were in this vicinity, but they didn't know our exact position. Further, we were not about to pinpoint our ambush position by firing a weapon and having our muzzle flash show them our location. I had my entrenching tool (small folding shovel) in hand with my arm back and ready and the others were equally armed and also ready to strike. Just as we were about to kill him, a voice out of the black whispered "Keepsake" or whatever the night's password was.

What the hell! One of us quickly and quietly said the correct response to him as we immediately understood that this guy was a friendly. "What the hell are you doing? You almost got yourself killed, you idiot," one of us shouted in a whisper. All four of our hearts were just now starting to pump again.

"I know, I know, I've been doing this for an hour," he said, "but the lieutenant wanted everyone to know that they've landed a man on the moon." Shit! We had a short discussion about how irrelevant, dangerous and stupid the courier's activities were and then he crawled through our location towards the next 3-man position.

I share this story because it is a great ambush story, and it illustrates the heightened senses and emotions experienced during an ambush. This is one of the few stories that I told when I was required to tell of my time in Nam. It was funny, short, and it demonstrated the fine edge between calm and action and rational and irrational behavior that was our daily life on-line.

However, as I conducted research for this book I discovered that, in fact, this really wasn't my story. For forty plus years I could see, hear, smell and touch that night. However, it turns out that it was not I who cocked the arm with that entrenching tool on July 20, 1969, because I was in the mortar platoon at that time. As near as I can figure, I was told that story by someone in Mike platoon two months after I was transferred to mortars, but I could imagine it happening so easily that I just absorbed it as my own story. I can still feel the tingles that permeated my body that night, but the dates just don't lie.

CHAPTER 12

LIFE IN THE FIELD

We would be in the field for two to three weeks before returning to a basecamp. While in the field, we would be resupplied every three to six days. When we finally did return to our basecamp, we would arrive late in the afternoon. We would then immediately get our field gear in order. This often meant resupplying or repairing equipment, receiving ammunition and any other required equipment for the field. We would never do any other activity until we were again ready for the field.

Then we would get our first shower (always cold) since our last time in basecamp, "new" clothes from the 90th and, finally, a hot meal. After all of this, we would sleep on army cots, which were absolute heaven to us. The next morning, we would be awakened at 4 a.m. or so and given a hot breakfast. After a rushed breakfast we would be driven out to the airstrip for an early morning airborne insertion into an LZ (landing zone) and then start the whole exhaustive hunt and kill cycle all over again. Overall, our life in the 1st Division was simple but brutal.

The daily life of a combat infantryman in the field was miserable. Our life consisted of trying to do the following: get dry or keep dry; cool down or warm up; be asleep or be very awake; drink very little water for fear of running out; and engage the enemy soundly and intelligently or make a mistake and become a statistic. Life was predictable, boring, very slow moving and then, BANG, the complete opposite.

Every day in the field would begin a half-hour before dawn, when all grunts would be awake and ready for an attack. If the

Mike Humlicek and Dwayne Ellrich find time to write letters on the bunkers between our sleeping tents. Note that the tents and bunkers are set up between the rubber tree rows.

enemy found our location during the night, they would usually assault at first light so they could see us. That fact required us to be ready and watch the sunrise every day. It wasn't as romantic as it sounds.

During the wet season, we would uncover ourselves by removing our poncho liners and crawl out of the puddles in which we were sleeping. A long night of sleeping in the rain was often cold, but if luck was with us, a puddle was in our position, and we would stay warmer if we slept in the puddle. After the "all ready" time, we would go out and retrieve and wrap up our claymore mines. We would then wring the water out of the poncho liner and spread it out on a bush; if it wasn't raining, it would be dry in fifteen minutes.

In the dry season, we would already be drenched in our own sweat just by moving enough to take in our claymores. At the same time, we might be heating something from our C rations. During the dry season (hot season) we were too hot and dry/thirsty to eat anything but our canned fruit, if we had any (we were usually rationed two cans per day).

During this time, our platoon leader would be talking by radio to our company CO as he was making plans for all three platoons for the day. Clear coordination was needed so that one platoon would not walk into one of the other well-armed platoons patrolling in the heavy jungle. The platoon leader would then meet with his point squad leader and develop a route for the day's mission. Next his squad leaders were called together, and the mission was passed down to them. "Saddle-up and move out" was announced, and we would move out in an orderly and secure manner to start our day of "searching and destroying."

Every four or five days, after we pulled in our claymores, the platoon would move out immediately and meet the other two platoons of our company. As the three platoons would gather, we would form into a large LZ and get prepared for being resupplied. The first chopper(s) would usually come in with a hot breakfast (in large metal coolers called Mermites), any needed ammo, mail, replacement soldiers, clean used uniforms (from the 90th Replacement) and men returning to the company from R and R (rest and relaxation). An R and R was a week's vacation to Taipei, Bangkok, Singapore, Hong Kong, Manila, Honolulu or Sydney. The squad leaders would organize their men to pick up and distribute the mail, uniforms and other supplies and then organize their men to go get breakfast. About 30 minutes later, the choppers would return and pick up the empty food containers, filthy uniforms to be burned back at the rear, and any soldiers that were going on R and R or going home after their year in Nam.

CHAPTER 13

C-RATIONS

A case of 12 C-Rations consisted of 12 different meals. These meals were categorized into three types; B-1, B-2 and B-3. Each case of rations contained four of each of these types. The contents varied a bit between types but the most important difference was that the B-1 and the B-3 had a nine-ounce can of fruit with each meal. Each squad leader would go to the supply line and made sure that each man would get a B-1, a B-2 and a B-3 for each day. This was critical in keeping the men in the squad happy because that ensured that each man received two cans of fruit daily and that each man got the same amount of food.

We would carry 4 or 5 days' food supply, which was heavy and noisy to carry. Every supply day would find men discarding much of their food because a number of the meals were just plain inedible. The only person I knew that could actually eat the canned scrambled eggs and ham meal was Mike Humlicek. There wasn't enough Tabasco in the world for most of us to eat that meal. Franks and beans was another meal that regularly was discarded. Humping 80 to100 pounds of gear is a chore, and we were always trying to find ways of lightening our loads. Pitching eggs and ham was an easy choice for lightening our loads.

If it was the dry season, we would throw away all of our food except the canned fruit and a tin of pound cake. The canned fruit gave us needed fluids and the pound cake was fairly good. We would start a fire and throw all of the unused food into it to make it inedible to the NVA. The trick was to use our p-38s (small can openers) to make a small opening for the steam to escape so the cans would not explode in the fire, and the contents would not scald a passing soldier. Almost every resupply day someone would forget to puncture a can (often someone new) and one or two cans would explode, pitching the super-heated contents onto a passerby. These became known as "peanut butter claymores." If you were hit by the contents, for several days you wore a badge of stupidity for having been unlucky enough to walk past a fire at the wrong time. Combat Infantry humor had strong portions of fate and cynicism.

During the dry season, we had a new First Sergeant that spent a few days out in the field with us (often they stayed in the rear for administrative purposes). He noticed that we were throwing away much of our issued food, and he didn't like seeing the food thrown into the fire and wasted. When he returned to the rear, he decided to issue only two meals for each soldier per day and thought that it would make very little difference. That decision had a negative impact on every soldier's food allotment in the company. Before that judgment every man got two cans of fruit every day; now when the squad leaders distributed the food some men would get more canned fruit than others during a resupply. The squad leader now had to make sure to remember who was shorted a fruit can so that he could even it out at the next resupply. The fruit was about all we ate, and that lifer cut our food intake by 33% by not understanding his men and their needs.

CHAPTER 14

PATROLLING

After we finished breaking up our ambush or our resupply, we would begin our day of patrolling. Most days we would start following our planned route and search for trails and the enemy. Typically we would hump for a couple of hours and then we would stop to perform a cloverleaf. We would also stop to cloverleaf if something abnormal was spotted by our point squad. During a clover-leaf, the main body of the platoon would form a circular defensive position and send out several squad leaders with three or four men each and patrol out to our left, right and to our front. These men would make a circle of up to 100 meters out, depending on the terrain, to spot and investigate something odd or just look for trails. After they returned, each squad leader would report what had been found to the platoon leader. If a tunnel, fresh grave, cave, unexploded artillery round or bomb, dead body or a thousand other distractions was found then we would explore it, dig it up, blow it up, investigate and bury it or in some way take care of it. Each day was an eternity.

If there was nothing to follow up, we would continue to follow our day's mission. This would be repeated over and over again until we either found some enemy to engage or prepare to set up an ambush. We were always thirsty, never trusting that we could find water or that we would be resupplied on time. We never stopped walking except for clover leafs or firefights. We were never dry because we were drenched from our own sweat or the monsoons. We rarely talked to each other because we were spread out or were following "silence discipline." We were never allowed a complete night's sleep in the field because we were awake one-third of the night on our watch. We were never allowed to drink any alcohol and relax when we came back in to base because we were always on "ready reserve" for our battalion. This meant that we could be called on to fly or run to the defense of a sister company at any time to help them in an overwhelming situation. We were never allowed to see a dentist, or go to the PX, go visit a friend in the basecamp or just get away from it all for an hour. We were always exhausted, pissed off, armed to the teeth, used to violence, treated like shit and were aware of all of this. No wonder they always kept us busy; no wonder there were so many "fraggings."

A fragging was an act where a soldier would attempt to kill another soldier, usually an uncaring lifer. In our battalion, fraggings were not racially motivated as in other places in Nam but were mostly directed against lifers. We heard that the First Sergeant who started issuing two meals a day instead of three, upon being promoted to be our battalion's Sergeant Major, was fragged several times over the next four or five months. Interestingly, he never received a scratch. We always thought that he was the luckiest son of a bitch in the army.

I recall one patrol during which we joined up with a company of mechanized infantry from our sister battalion, the 2nd of the 2nd Infantry. We all were going into an area where there were known basecamps and we were going to need both the extra firepower of the mechanized troop carriers and the flexibility and manpower of the ground based infantry for this region.

So for us straight (not mechanized) infantry of A½, that meant that we rode on top of the M113 "tracks" as the track crews slowly broke trails through the jungle and bamboo forests, looking for basecamps. For those of us sitting on top, it was like breaking a wild horse for twelve or more hours a day. All day I just kept resetting my machine gun upright and readjusting it so it wouldn't fall off the track. I just hung onto any part of the track that I could grip with both of my hands.

When the inevitable firefights started, I would grab my machine gun, jump off the track and head for the fighting. If the firefight was in a section other than Mike Platoon's, we would organize and prepare to begin a supportive tactic of some kind.

M113 (Courtesy commons.wikipedia.org.)

This joint operation proceeded for two or three days over which we continued to slowly build up our enemy body count.

The front of the M113s that we were using was shaped with a flat vertical plane on the bottom half and an approximately 45° backward sloping plane on the top half. At the break line of these two planes was a continuous piano style hinge that was attached to the front of the track and onto a stout piece of plywood that was slightly smaller in size than the sloping metal surface of the track. This configuration allowed the plywood to be either folded up next to the front of the track against the metal or folded away from the track forming a forward angled 45° plane. When it was locked away from the front it formed an angled plane that directed water away from the top of the track when it would ford a deep stream acting much as a prow on a boat. As the body count was increasing, the space formed between the plywood prow and the backward sloping front was being used on several M113s as storage for the enemy dead.

Normally we in A½ left our enemy dead behind after we searched them for any intelligence, but for some reason the men of the 2nd of the 2nd, at least on this mission, were stacking the bodies on the front of their tracks.

Meanwhile, some big cheese thought this would be a great operation in which to have a newsman join us for a few days to see our soldiers in action. I never saw him but he spent parts of two days interviewing officers and men and taking pictures of different parts of our operation. Early morning on the fourth day of our mission we were resupplied by air and then we split from the 2nd of the 2nd. We next started our normal platoon-sized patrol and ambush routine. I think that the correspondent flew back with those supply ships. As we separated from the 2nd of the 2nd we never gave the incident another thought.

Several weeks later, there was natter that the company of the 2nd of the 2nd was under investigation for desecrating dead enemy bodies. I heard from the gossip that, while the correspondent took pictures of the bodies of the dead NVA soldiers that were stacked on the front of the M113s, he noticed that as the track pushed through the jungle, sometimes heavier brush and small trees would force the top of the plywood back and pinch the bodies a bit. There were not many bodies on any single track, and no bodies were damaged that I saw since the plywood seldom if ever passed the vertical plane of the steel front of the M113. However, that didn't stop the absurd furor about our conduct in the field. I know that the track's crew members didn't want those bodies on the track since they were only an annoyance to them, but someone higher up wanted to collect the bodies. Most of us grunts thought that the best course of action would be to have the investigators go jump in the shit of the senior officer that had wanted the photo op of the body count for his promotion file. Against the truly gruesome backdrop of our daily life the investigation of this insignificant squishing incident seemed farcical to us and oh so typical of how far removed the powers were from the reality of the war and from the men that fought the war.

CHAPTER 15

THE LIFE OF A "NEWBIE"

"Everything is funny as long as it is happening to somebody else."
—Will Rogers, *The Illiterate Digest* (1924)

This dismal daily routine was preceded by a steep learning curve. A new grunt needed to learn lots of little bits, fragments and chunks of information to keep alive and sane. Every newbie entered into an overwhelming new world. First, nothing in training had prepared anyone for the conditioning required just to do the necessary daily walking out in the field. It was hotter, more humid and often hillier than anything we had experienced in training. Moreover, we all had much more weight in equipment to carry than we had previously faced in any training situation. Just knowing how far apart to walk in a column was a challenge; it depended on the terrain, the density of the jungle and sometimes even the time of day.

In the very thickest jungle, you could lose the man in front of you in twenty seconds. In those heavy jungles, there were thin, wispy vines with thorns as big and hard as rose thorns. These thorns had very sharp barbs on them that hooked your arms or eyelid or clothes, and it would take thirty or forty-five seconds to unhook them. In that time the man in front of you was long gone. In that jungle one didn't just yell to find the column again.

Rather, we would quietly call "wait a minute" to the fellow in front, hoping that he would slow up his pace a bit and have the fellow in front of him do the same, and so on. Then the column would stretch out and not get separated because of that vine. In GI language that plant was called the Wait-a-Minute vine.

* * *

An entire two-column formation could come to a halt if someone unluckily bumped into a red ant nest and became covered with red ants. The ants were large and red and they inflicted incredibly painful bites that caused excruciating pain as dozens of them paid the soldier his due for disturbing the nest. Often a soldier would almost strip naked to shake and brush off the ants. It was not unusual for the medic to have to pour alcohol or peroxide in the soldier's ear to remove some biting ants that were inside. Those ants were one of the most despised parts of our lives.

* * *

A newbie was often the victim of old timers' pranks. Jimmy White, my assistant gunner, and I sometimes would give a newbie (our ammo bearer was always a newbie) some C-4 explosive to heat his C rations. When heating C Rations, the top of the can was opened almost the entire way around the can but then the top was folded back so that the lid became a handle. The C-4 burned at a very high temperature and almost always the intense heat from the C-4 would cause the moisture at the bottom of the can to instantly turn to steam and force the entire contents of food in the can to rise up in the can and fall out on the ground if one didn't stir it. All that was necessary to distract the newbie enough to make that happen was to get him to talk about home, and he would always forget about watching his food. Then, when he looked back at his food, it would be on the ground. We would laugh, teach him to stir his food and throw him a can of something else to eat.

* * *

When I was a newbie, I can clearly recall the first time that we newbies came across a civilian that was selling Seiko watches.

Jim Gray cleaning his M16

We couldn't believe our eyes. The local showed us these gorgeous, polished, stylish and so very, very inexpensive watches. "Wow, I want to buy two of those beauties!" we all said. "Don't be bigger fools than you already are," said the few old timers that even gave a shit enough to say anything to us. "They're shit." Everyone took the sage advice about the watches except good old Mike Humlicek. He and his big eyes just couldn't pass up those bargains.

We all trusted the old guys and told Mike that he would be sorry. He just scoffed at us and said that he was the smart one. As days passed he continued to praise the watch, himself and his wisdom. Then came the first night of the monsoon season. Mike woke up the next morning and noticed his watch had stopped. "That jerk sold me a faulty self-winder," said Mike. "Bullshit," said one of the old timers, "it's full of rust; they always are." Mike couldn't believe it. He kept telling everybody that it kept perfect time as he pulled out his knife and popped off the back. The entire contents of the watch case were covered with very fine rust—every gear, every bracket and even the spring. Mike just stood there with wide disbelieving eyes, cocked his arm back and threw the watch as far into the jungle as he could: "Son-of-a-bitch."

I had been on-line in Vietnam for less than a week, and already I understood there was only one certainty—there were many things to learn just to survive and I wasn't learning them fast enough. I was in a three-man position on the kill zone of a night ambush on a fresh trail (one showing recent activity). One of the more experienced men in the group was awake on his 2 ½ hour watch, and my watch was coming up. I needed to sleep, but I just couldn't fall off. Suddenly about ten to fifteen feet in front of me I heard a frighteningly loud sound. "RRHHHHRR, RRHHHRR, RRHHHRR... Fuck You, Fuck You, Fuck You!" I thought, "Holy shit, an enemy is right out in front of my position, behind the kill zone! That NVA fucker is taunting me and trying to scare me into revealing my exact position." I had never been so awake in my life. I must have gasped involuntarily because immediately I heard a very soft chuckle coming from the guy on watch right next to me! What the hell...!?

The old timers would always chuckle softly at the sheer terror that a newbie would feel in the total darkness of an ambush the first time he heard the "Fuck You Lizard." The FY Lizard was a smallish gecko lizard that would become active at night. It would crow/growl three times and then say "fuck you" three times, as clearly as if it were a person. The first time most newbies heard it at night, alone and in an ambush, it was absolutely terrifying. The old timers always hoped that it would happen on their watch so they could hear the newbie gasp. The other old timers would keep right on sleeping and never even hear the noise.

* * *

"Hey, Beed," said my machine gunner in a heavy Mississippi drawl. "If I were you I would move." It was mid-morning and I was a newbie, maybe two or three weeks on-line, and I was exhausted. I was humping ammo (two cans of M60 rounds), and we had just stopped for a platoon cloverleaf. I had just collapsed against a rice paddy dike, and so I asked him if I should have been further or closer to him or should I be on top or the other side of the dike or had I done some other thing wrong? He just looked at me and said that if he were I, he would put more distance between that very poisonous snake and himself. I never sat down again without a quick but thorough scan for snakes, spiders, red ants or NVA tricks.

* * *

Song Be was typical of another fact of our life—rats. Song Be, Quan Loi, Lai Khe and the rest of our basecamps were old. They had all been built during the early military buildup in 1965 and 1966. There was a well-known correlation between the age of the basecamp and the rat population of the camp. Whenever it was necessary for us to be in bunkers at night to sleep, such as during a night of persistent incoming, rats would crawl over us regularly. One way to control them was to have just a little bit of light in the bunker. If we had a candle to burn, that was enough light to keep them out of our bunker. Often, though, we couldn't find a candle or it created too much heat in the bunker and we couldn't sleep.

One night when I was in Mike Platoon, I was in Song Be overnight. Mike Platoon was out in the field and another company from our battalion was on the bunker line, so I didn't know anyone. Our mortar platoon was at Song Be, and I knew a few guys there so I was hanging out with them until I caught a chopper to join my company in the field the next morning. Since there were no fortified sleeping quarters in Song Be, we were sleeping on the ground near some fighting bunkers to roll into when our usual nightly incoming mortars started coming in. Everyone that wasn't firing counter-fire back at the enemy crawled into the bunkers until the incoming stopped and we then continued our sleeping outside.

That night was an unusual night in that in a few more minutes the incoming returned. This pattern persisted, and I finally decided to sleep in the bunker so I could sleep straight through until morning. That was a luxury for me. As I was sleeping, rats kept running across my lower legs and then would run out the bunker door. Finally I got tired of that and turned 90 degrees so that my body was parallel to their route. I was sleeping on my back, and the move seemed to have been a smart one when all of a sudden a rat ran up on my face, paused and the scurried off into the darkness. I can still feel his ratty feet and claws on my face and lips. "OK that's it. I'm sleeping outside and fuck the incoming," I silently shouted as I crawled out into the starlight.

CHAPTER 16

UNWRITTEN RULES

There were many informal routines and unwritten rules that dictated behavior in our platoon. For example, one day we were patrolling and had stopped for a cloverleaf. During these times the main part of the platoon, including both gun crews, would form a defensive position consisting of three-man positions forming a circle about 20 meters in diameter.

Jimmy White, my assistant gunner and I were sitting behind a small natural berm and looking outward when we both heard a scratching sound in the underbrush just on the other side of the berm. Someone had to peek his head over the berm and see what was making the noise. Custom dictated that whoever

Jimmy White (r) with Leon Gaston

nodded to the other person first was not the one that had to do the peeking. Damn, Jimmy was quicker and I had to take a look.

The damn scratching continued and seemed to be moving; I had to take a look now. So I took off my pot (steel helmet) and slowly raised my head to look over. The noise had stopped as if the culprit were listening, too. Up, up my neck stretched, and—I was looking eyeball to eyeball with an up-stretched peacock.

Many times, wild peafowl did not get spooked if our patrols would walk by them. I imagine this guy had heard us all quietly come in and just kept grazing. But he moved toward our three man position as he continued to graze and he eventually roamed over to within hearing distance of our spot.

I burst out in a stifled laugh and lowered my head. “What, what?” asked Jimmy. I told him that it was a peacock and all three of us, including the peacock, quietly laughed our asses off.

CHAPTER 17

THE CASTE SYSTEM

"When one treats people with benevolence, justice, and righteousness and reposes confidence in them, the army will be united in mind and all will be happy to serve their leaders."
—Sun Tzu

Life in the "Big Red One," historic army slang for the First Infantry Division, in 1968-69 was tough because of our mission, but life in general was even more miserable in the draft infantry because it was a two-caste system. There were the lifers and the grunts. The lifers included any officer that had the rank of Captain or above, some Staff Sergeants (with rank of E6), all Sergeants First Class (with rank of E7) and all sergeants above. These guys were the upper caste, and the grunts were the very lowest caste.

The lifers had all the power, benefits, and perks. The grunts had nothing but responsibility and misery. The lifers' positions were that of leadership but most of them were not good leaders; they were takers. Characteristics of good military leaders commonly include the following: competence, honesty, integrity, courage, ability to inspire, good communication skills and a desire to support their people in accomplishing their mission as competently and safely as possible

Most of our lifer leaders were total calamities as leaders. There was never any kind of communication, support, inspiration or any other leadership quality expressed to us by most of our lifer chain of command. Instead they simply made our lives busy, exhausting and dangerous.

We had three Commanding Officers (all captains) during my year in A ½. The first one we all respected in the field, but he didn't mingle with his troops. I never spoke a single word to him. The second one was a disaster in every way, causing a very high body count among our own soldiers because of his stupidity. He was reviled by all of us. The second one was relieved from command in a quiet way a few weeks after we got decimated (more about that later). We were all glad to see him go because we had endured a number of senseless casualties in the field because of him. But here is the irony: he was relieved after the huge loss of men in the company. Yet, the decision to take back our own bunkers at such a high casualty rate had not been his decision. It came from the battalion commander over the radio, but it was the tactical leadership of the company CO that night that got so many men killed and wounded. I never met or saw the third CO that we had. By then I was in mortars, and he never once came to our area or called anyone other than the platoon sergeant to see him. I heard later from the men in the rifle platoons that he was a very good CO. He treated the men well and even gave them a day or so off between missions to rest a bit.

The only conversation I ever had with any of our COs in my year tour was with the second one. We had a three-sentence conversation when he asked me if I wanted him to transfer me to mortars. My COs were not much for knowing their troops.

In my estimation, only 10% of the lifers had any care or concern about the men that they had in their command. SSG Wright , FSG Wingate and perhaps my third CO were part of the 10% exception. The other 90% were in the war to make rank for themselves at any cost! To make rank, a lifer had to distinguish himself from others by displaying bold leadership. The result for the grunts was being volunteered for mission after mission of questionable merit. We were kept in an exhausted state. We were always strung out and exposed. The result was often missions that were mind-bogglingly stupid and costly but that were daring with the hope of attracting some higher lifer's attention. There was NO accountability for lives lost in the draft infantry.

CHAPTER 18

THE INFANTS IN THE INFANTRY

By 1968 at the height of the war and the draft many of the grunts were only 19. Typically a man would turn 18 and graduate high school by June, not be in college in September and therefore be classified as active 1A by October or November. He would be drafted by December, have two months of basic and two months of infantry training, three to four weeks of leave and would be in the Vietnamese bush by June. In contrast, the average age for a grunt in World War II was 25. Few infantrymen in Vietnam had any education beyond high school, and some hadn't graduated at all. I was 2 ½ years older than most men because I had worked one semester and had gone to college for two years. That made enough difference that I was often call Gramps or Dad because I was 21, in Nam and in the infantry. I was in a part of an army in which most grunts had very little life experience before they were required to spend 12 months hunting and killing people.

Life was hell in 1968-69. The lifers were running up the promotion points, the draft machinery was running smoothly for replacements, and the grunts were being turned into killers and cannon fodder.

CHAPTER 19

FLYING INTO THE FIELD

Let me insert a bit of First Infantry historical, logistical and tactical background. In 1968-69 the 1st Infantry Division was an Air Mobile Division. That meant that we would almost always use helicopters for aerial insertions into the field. Seldom were we entering a neutral area, and because there were often few open areas in the thick vegetation, we would frequently land into the same LZ several times. It was not uncommon for the LZ to be hot (with enemy fire directed at the incoming aircraft and soldiers).

When we flew into the field, we always flew in the entire company. After we landed, we would then usually split into our platoons and begin our customary search and destroy missions.

The physics and logistics of the flights were as follows. Each UH-1 Huey transport helicopter (Slick) could carry six regular riflemen into an LZ. However, if a radioman (RTO) or an M60 machine gun crew were aboard then the extra weight of these soldiers would reduce the number to only five men on the aircraft (see weight chart below). In determining the makeup of the *first wave flights* these rules would be followed:

1. One M60 machine gun crew must be included for the all-important initial firepower, 5 men on this chopper.
2. One platoon sergeant or lieutenant, along with RTO (radio operator) must be included for the leadership and communications, 5 men on this chopper.

3. As many riflemen as possible were placed on the remaining choppers, 6 men on these choppers.
4. As many choppers as possible were acquired for the insertion (usually three to five).

In the pre-dawn darkness, we would wait on a base airstrip for our choppers to arrive for the aerial insertion. Only a part of the company could be flown on these assigned choppers for the first wave; the rest of the company would follow in successive waves. We were all hoping or praying for six choppers and we were always disappointed when only four or five choppers flew in. Each additional wave would follow the first into the LZ, and it usually took from 20 minutes to one hour for a chopper to complete a round trip. Three choppers in a wave meant the arrival of 16 men (five+five+six), four choppers meant the arrival of 22 men (five+five+six+six) and five choppers resulted in 27 or 28 men (five+five+six+six+six or five).

The men on the first wave had to establish control of the entire LZ area. So if that LZ was hot, the men of the first wave would begin suppressing the enemy fire in the area and move

(Courtesy pixabay.com.)

out to try and secure an area of about 150 feet by 50 feet. That was often an impossible feat for 16 men in a hot LZ. We often had to call for gunship cover if things were perilous in the beginning.

In Alpha Company, Mike Platoon (mine) was the "go to" platoon because we had Staff Sergeant (SSG) Wright. He was the best Platoon Sergeant (in fact he was the best soldier) in our company. Therefore we were rotated into being assigned as the first flight into an LZ more often than Lima or November Platoons. I was the machine gun squad leader so my gun crew was usually the crew that was assigned to the first wave. Immediately after landing, we needed to concentrate our heavy fire power (the machine gun) towards the bulk of the enemy fire and somehow protect our flanks and rear over a large area, using only the 16 or 22 men from the first wave, while waiting for the next wave to fly in. Sometimes the time between waves seemed like days, not minutes.

For me, landing in a hot LZ meant jumping out of the chopper and running towards the part of the tree line with the most intense enemy fire and beginning to place suppressing fire to that area. The M60 machine gun was the priority target for the NVA. There was no way to hide or camouflage the M60 so they knew exactly where to direct their fire—at me. The RTO (radio) was the second priority target and it too was impossible to camouflage. It was never fast or easy to run anywhere humping more than eighty to a hundred pounds (as the machine gunner, radio operator and others did) especially running through who knows what terrain. We would do our best to secure the LZ and with each successive incoming wave it got less hectic and safer.

The minimum gear that we took into the field varied from person to person depending on his assigned position and responsibility.

I have a confession to make here; I often carried an empty holster into the field so you can subtract about five pounds from my machine gunner load for the missing 45-caliber pistol. Whenever it was discovered during inspection that I had an empty holster, my Platoon Leader would order a new 45, magazine and ammo from supply for me. When the items would arrive, almost always they would be short of either the magazine or the 45 ammo. Very few times did I have a complete 45 caliber

Minimum Basic Combat Load For Each Man

The following is the *minimum* weight each common soldier would be carrying the first day of an operation or after being resupplied in the bush.

Item	Weight in Pounds
2 Fragmentation Grenades	2
4 Smoke grenades	6
Water – 5 quarts	10
C Rations – 5 days' supply	25
M-18 Claymore Mine	4
M-1 Helmet and liner	4
Entrenching Tool – Small Shovel	5 (Every 3rd Man)
Total Basic Load	56 pounds

This minimum weight does not include web gear, uniform, and personal items. Each soldier then added the weight of the gear required for his assigned responsibility.

Item	Weight in Pounds
Machine gunner: M60 machine gun, 100+ round starter belt, 45-caliber pistol, entrenching tool	56+39 = 95 pounds
Assistant Gunner/Ammo Bearer: M16, 10 loaded magazines, rucksack frame with 2 cans (400 rounds) of M60 ammo (no entrenching tool)	56+43 = 97 pounds
Radio Operator (RTO): PRC25 radio w/ battery, an additional battery, extra antennas, M16 rifle, 10 loaded magazines (no entrenching tool)	56+54 = 110 pounds
Rifleman: M16, 20 loaded magazines. (Note: many riflemen had additional loads such as 20 pounds of C-4 for the demolition man or the platoon's Starlight scope; then the total would be 98 pounds)	56+32 = 88 pounds

pistol. I was not about to carry ANY extra weight, so if it was not a functional weapon I would slowly take the 45 apart in the field and throw the pieces into the bush over a day or two and over multiple miles. I couldn't leave it behind; I had nowhere to keep it until the missing ammo or magazine caught up to me, so I just got rid of the weight.

CHAPTER 20

MOVEMENT IN THE FIELD

Before I talk about platoon movement, here is a brief explanation about the leadership terminology used in an infantry line company:

- Company Commander or Commanding Officer (CO). He was usually a captain and a Lifer (although for a short period of time a 1st Lieutenant might fill in). He was in command of all three rifle platoons (Lima, Mike and November) and the Mortar platoon. He was usually in the field with one of the three platoons. He planned the company's overall strategy in the field for each extended mission and would assign and coordinate each platoon's daily work area. He would be in radio contact with each platoon leader throughout the day. I never liked it when he was with our platoon in the field; it just seemed more confusing with both the CO and the platoon leader. I was always pleased to see him take off with Lima or November when we would split up to begin our patrols. He reported to the Battalion Commander.
- Platoon Leader. This was a 1st Lieutenant's position but was often filled by the senior sergeant in the platoon because of a shortage of lieutenants. He commanded the platoon and directed all of the platoon's activities in the field. The lieutenants were usually not lifers but were

OCS or ROTC graduates. Many of these were not competent alone, at least not at first, but survived by working with their senior NCOs (non-commissioned officers or senior sergeants) and others (point squad leader and his RTO). Just like all of us, most would improve with time on-line. The lieutenants reported to the CO.

- Platoon Sergeant. This was a Staff Sergeant (SSG E-6) or Sergeant First Class (SFC E-7) position. These ranks were usually lifer positions but were seldom filled by these men because of a critical shortage of these ranks. Ordinarily they were the second in command of the platoon and because they were located at the rear of the platoon, they directed the troop movements at the rear of the platoon during firefights (see below about troop movements in the field).
- Squad leader. This is a Sergeant's slot but was often filled by a Specialist 4th Class (Spec 4). These men were in charge of four to six men and would lead their men as directed by the Platoon Leader or Platoon Sergeant. They were also responsible for their squad's supplies, food, mail and assigned tasks. They would report to the Platoon Leader. I was the squad leader for Mike Platoon's machine gun squad.

Next I will provide the reader with some basic information about the mechanics of platoon movement in the field. When we moved through the terrain, we always moved in two columns which were spaced about 10 to 30 feet apart depending on the terrain. Each platoon had four squads: a point squad of five or six men, two rifle squads of four to six men each and a machine gun squad made up of two gun crews of three. The point squad was split between the two columns and provided the first two or three men in the front of each column; the squad leader had an RTO. Next, in the opposite column of the point squad leader was the Platoon Leader, with his RTO. All platoon radios were tuned to the company net or frequency. Next in the column was one of the machine gun crews. Finally the rest of the column would be men from one of the rifle squads. The last man would be paying close attention to all things to the rear of the moving column.

Lt. Pratt and SSG Wright

In the other column behind the point squad would be most of the men from the other rifle squad followed by the other gun crew. Following them would be the platoon sergeant and his RTO, followed by a man from the rifle squad as a rear guard. The platoon's medic would fall in anywhere he wanted to but was usually centrally located.

This formation had leadership towards the front and back as well as to the left and right of the platoon. The same could be said for the firepower from the platoon's machine guns. We had our best point people up front rotating time on-point; this kept them fresh and more effective.

The two-column formation allowed maximum firepower to be established in a very short time. If the point squad walked into a firefight, we would quickly scramble riflemen from each column to the front and spread out parallel to the enemy front. We could continue to do this until most riflemen and both big guns were involved in the firefight. The platoon sergeant would stay back with a few riflemen to secure our rear and flanks. If we were attacked from the rear exactly the same thing would happen but in reverse. If we were hit on one of our flanks, many of the men in the column not being engaged would immediately be directed across the formation and integrated into the opposite column to engage in the firefight. Meanwhile our new flanks and rear would be covered.

The platoon leader's radio operator would typically be used as the pace man. His job was to count his steps and keep the platoon leader advised how far we had traveled from the last point he had reported. This information was then used to locate our position on our maps. The same process was being used in the point squad. These two maps would be reconciled several times a day. In heavy vegetation, it was oftentimes very difficult to determine our exact location. On several occasions that situation led to inaccurate artillery support. In my opinion, modern GPS tracking and artillery systems are the greatest improvements for the grunt since the time that I was humping.

CHAPTER 21

A STORY ABOUT LIFE IN THE FIELD— AND DEATH

Some days just seemed to go on and on, fueled by one disaster after another. One day the company landed into an LZ without incident. Jimmy and I had a FNG (fucking new guy) assigned as our ammo bearer, which was common. For some reason, we stayed together as a company in the field and we started to patrol with Mike Platoon last in line, following Lima and November Platoons. We eventually came to a river and the CO sent small parties to recon up and down both banks for several hundred meters. We were going to cross the river at this fairly shallow portion and we didn't want to have enemy fire from the river banks at the time we were most vulnerable.

Just before we started to the river, one of the teams spotted a few tunnels slightly upstream from us, so the company was formed into a defensive position around the tunnels. Mike platoon formed the extreme downstream part of the circle with my gun on the bank with a field of fire both down our river bank and across the river to the bank on the other side.

The company spent over an hour exploring the tunnels but found nothing in them. So the CO decided to continue the patrol across the river. The company then started to cross over, and my gun crew covered their flank up and across the river. Little did my crew know but the CO had told my lieutenant to have Mike Platoon fill all of the tunnels with CS (tear gas) before we left the area to cross over the river.

What a stupid order. The CS had no lasting effect on the long term use of the tunnel so it was just a waste of materials. However it was a disaster for me and my crew. We held our position until most of Mike Platoon was in the river and as we prepared to move out and bring up the rear of the formation the CS started to roll out of the tunnels and spread through the bush. The men had not been skimpy with the CS, and it soon had the entire jungle between us and the river crossing spot totally impassable. Every passing minute was separating us from our platoon and the company.

As we were waiting for the gas to diminish, we reviewed a couple of the very first rules we learned pertaining to correct behavior in the bush. One, a person does not yell loudly in the jungle to draw attention, especially when the problem is that you are alone and detached from your group. Two, one does not run to catch up with the rest of the boys because that makes noise and movement behind an armed and alert group that isn't expecting anything good rushing up to them from behind.

The gas finally dissipated enough for us to make it through to the crossing area. The three of us quickly and quietly crossed the river, went up a steep bank and started to catch up to the platoon. We had gone a hundred yards or so when we saw our platoon sergeant and a couple of men coming back towards us.

The sergeant had done his head count after the crossing and found us missing. It had taken 100 meters or so to radio the leading platoon and stop the company so that he could come back and make contact with us. Man, were we glad to see him; it sure made the reuniting with the company easier and safer for us.

Later that day the company was spread out in two columns trudging up a long, open, up-sloping area two or three thousand meters long. I had never seen such a wide open area in Nam. Maybe the old man (CO) was surprised by the open area too because the word soon came down that the three platoons were to form into three platoon formations side-by-side, abandoning our existing two-column formation. So soon there were six shorter columns side-by-side. He then had each platoon separate a bit, forming three pairs of shorter columns.

The buzz was that he wanted to watch each platoon implement basic fire and maneuver technique. These tactics allow movement towards the enemy while under fire, by having half the soldiers firing towards the enemy, suppressing the enemy's fire, while the other half is running forward a prescribed distance to some cover. Then they in turn would lay down covering fire for the other half so that they could advance. These maneuvers are easier said than done and a bit of practice wouldn't hurt.

So the three platoons got in a line, spread out side by side, and started performing fire and maneuver techniques running up the slope. We were all practicing our maneuvering when suddenly a sniper started shooting some rounds at us. We all suspected that it was just a solitary enemy that was assigned to keep track of us in the field, but just couldn't resist firing at us. Who could resist shooting a few rounds at a bunch of people out in a wide open space and lined up like a bunch of fools? He would get behind some cover about 700-800 yards away and pop off a few rounds at us. He wasn't very accurate at that range, but he was safe.

All of our fire was then directed to his position, but by that time, he was long gone to another place. Then he'd pop off a few more rounds and move on. He did this about three or four times and Company A diligently continued to perform our fire and maneuver techniques for our CO.

During one of the times when our machine gun crew finished our firing cycle, the other half of our platoon started firing and my crew started running forward under the safety of the covering fire. When we had run a distance and thrown ourselves down to get ready to begin to fire again, Jimmy and I noticed that our ammo bearer wasn't with us. We looked back and saw that he was still lying down back at the place that we had just come from. We were all exhausted from our running but we both muttered something like "the FNG needs to get in shape."

Jimmy threw me a couple of belts of ammo and ran back to kick that kid's butt. In a minute or two the fire and maneuver was stopped and I looked back to see how Jimmy and the ammo bearer were doing. What did I see? Our lieutenant, the medic and others were kneeling in the area around Jimmy. Soon Jimmy ran back and told me that the kid had a hole in his pot (steel helmet) right in the middle of his forehead. He was dead as a doornail.

Well, we all knew that the sniper was not targeting the ammo bearer; he was firing at the M60 (easily identifiable by the tracer rounds) as the priority target. But he fired wide-left of me and hit the new guy. Life and death were often determined by randomness and not skill or maneuver.

The CO assigned one platoon to go chase the sniper away and had the rest of us set up an LZ for the medevac chopper. We all did our jobs, and within an hour, all three platoons were back together and ready to move out on patrols. Jimmy and I got a different FNG and started to move out. Jimmy and I had never even had time to learn that new kid's name.

* * *

The everyday life of an infantry soldier has been absolutely miserable in every American war, and there will always be a bit of a brotherhood in that shared suffering and martyrdom. As to the quality of life, I must agree with the wisdom of my preceding grunts. Many combat veterans repeat this old combat axiom: "War is long periods of boredom punctuated by moments of sheer terror."

PART 4

LAI KHE

CHAPTER 22

THE SLICK

The UH1D helicopter, or "Slick" to us, was the heartbeat of the Airmobile Infantryman in Vietnam. We could not have existed without it. When we were in the field it was our exclusive transportation to the enemy, our resupply vehicle, ambulance, supplier of emergency ammo and supplies and it was our sweet ride back to basecamp. From the day it took us to our company for our first day in the field to the final ride out to begin our return home it was an endless, relentless, incessant companion.

I clearly remember one night when I had been in-country three or four months. We were on an ambush when I realized

The ever-present Slick (Courtesy commons.wikipedia.org.)

that there was never a time, day or night, that I didn't hear the sound of a slick. I have no idea how far those sounds travel in the heavy forested areas and jungles that I lived in. I only knew that the distant buzz was always there. To me now, the sound and smell of a slick is my nearest and quickest trigger to life in Vietnam.

It was the beginning of another mission and Lima, Mike and November platoons were on the basecamp's airstrip in the predawn darkness; A Company was again going out into the field. This was always my toughest time on-line. We would be sitting quietly, focusing on the many scenarios that could take place in the next hour. We would silently review a reaction to every possible situation that we could think might happen. It took all of my courage just to sit there and wait for the pending pickup and insertion. It took much more courage than it took when we were actually reacting to threats.

All of us were listening for the sound of approaching slicks. Then we recognized those sounds as they finally started getting louder. First it was the distant buzz of them, and then it was the growl of the turbine along with the thumping of the blades, and eventually it was the thunderous WHOP, WHOP as they came towards us to pick us up and begin the three-week cycle of our tense and exhausting hell.

Now the slicks were upon us, our crouching bodies looking away from them as they hurled sand, dust and pebbles at us. The familiar stink of JP4, lubricants and diesel was in the air and then here they were, ships with no cargo doors so nothing was in the way of us getting on and off with ease. I never saw a supply slick with doors on it in our division. Then "Move out," came the command, and we would squint, crouch and dash towards the gaping square holes in the side of the ship. We would throw anything we were holding onto the floor and then hop on our butts to slide onto the edge of the floor. Jimmy and I would always sit so that I would be ahead of him when we dismounted; that way he would never lose sight of me as we charged towards the gunfire on the ground. We grabbed onto flush mounted cargo rings built into the floor as we swung our over-laden legs into the beast. Within seconds, we all felt the increased pulsations as the slick's nose simultaneously moved forward and down as it took off. These were the times that we were the most pumped, high on emotions and adrenalin as we were going in, and the slick was merciless as it delivered us to hell.

Five days later, all three platoons in the field would gather together an hour after daybreak to once again honor the slick. We were now gathering for our resupply ritual. Once more we were listening for the sounds of arriving slicks, but this time with a more agreeable viewpoint. It was bringing us a hot breakfast of bacon and hot powdered eggs in Mermite insulated containers along with dry toast, coffee and orange juice. Word from the "world" in the form of mail would be on-board, as well as fresh water, cases of all kinds of cigarettes used for smoking or as barter and cases of C-rations to fuel the company for the next stretch of days. Clean hand-me-down jungle fatigues and batteries for the radios were also brought out to us every time. Also, it would be the taxi back to the basecamp for a couple of lucky soldiers that got to escape hell for a week on their only out-of-country R and R. Unfortunately, this merciless slick also delivered a couple of men returning from their R and R back into our nightmare so they could begin counting days on their long stretch to going home. Now that they had finished their R and R there was nothing else to look forward to except going home.

Soon we would have everything distributed, picked up, burned or thrown back on the slick and we would hear them fade away as each platoon would leave the area on a different heading as we began our own search-and-destroy routines once more. Then the only sounds were of us breaking jungle and the constant sound of distant slicks.

When we made heavy contact, we would always welcome the comforting sound of a different helicopter, the AH-1 Cobra attack helicopter. The sound meant we had a great ally on our side with enormous firepower. It would often make an enemy force break contact with us or would keep in check a superior force until the battle shifted in our favor. The sound of the Cobra was familiar to us because the Cobra was a close mechanical cousin to the slick. It was developed using the engine, transmission and rotor system of the slick and they sounded remarkably similar. During a firefight, we heard and felt those familiar sounds punctuated with the roar of the mini-gun, rockets and belt-fed

Cobra Gunship, the "skinny slick." (Courtesy en.wikipedia.org.)

grenade launcher. All of these weapons were game changers for us, and we always loved those skinny slicks.

If we were unlucky in the fight and sustained casualties, we relied once again on the slick but this time to perform acts of compassion. This time they had doors and Red Crosses on them. These were Medevac choppers. After waiting an eternity for them to arrive, we all used all of our will power to have them get down fast and safely. These were the most important slicks—these were literally life savers.

The senior RTO would call the Medevac chopper in and a number of FNGs would assist the Medevac attendant in loading the casualties after the platoon medic prioritized the wounded. KIAs would sometimes be loaded on the Medevac or sometimes be loaded on emergency resupply choppers if we ordered them. After the scurried activity on the LZ, the doors would be slid shut as the chopper was flying away.

These Medevacs would come as soon as they could, even during a firefight. They would come in conditions in which some other choppers would hesitate. In one of our worst night firefights, two of these incredible machines and crews hovered just over the top of the jungle to lower through the heavy canopy special cages (jungle penetrators) to winch up our wounded. They were very clear targets, yet each hovered and hoisted a number of critically wounded for evacuation to our Aid Station. We were in awe of them, yet we never got to thank them since they were stationed in other basecamps. Thank you now!

Cooling off and going in! (Courtesy en.wikipedia.org.)

We endured endless patrols, endless ambushes and endless days. Every chance I got to close my eyes there was the low buzz of the distant slicks. How could there be so many? Then one day soft rumors would start that maybe we were going back to basecamp in one or two days. With that idea out there, the days turned agonizingly long. Those damned RTOs; they knew just enough to make our lives miserable with their loose talk. With a break in sight, the ambushes felt twice as long as we wished for daybreak and a chance to fly back to basecamp. Each day seemed longer, but we were hopeful to meet soon with the other platoons to form an LZ for those beautiful slicks. "Please don't extend our time out here," we all would hope.

Finally the afternoon would arrive when the word came down that we were meeting with the rest of the company and we were to fly back to the basecamp. Our loads seemed about half the weight as we were directed to our sector of the LZ. Upbeat, my crew and I would set up a firing position for our gun and wait for me (as the Machine Gun Squad Leader) to get the word to go see the Platoon Leader. Here I would receive our platoon's order of withdrawal.

Next we mostly just waited and wished for a speedy pickup. Sometimes if we had had some contact in the last few days, I would start my equipment replacement list just to save my time in basecamp, but mostly we just listened to the distant buzz of the slicks and hoped to hear the beautiful sounds of approaching ones. Once they arrived, there was an organized system of placing a maximum number of men together to jump onboard each chopper. That ritual was so anticipated and practiced that the choppers barely stopped and never touched down.

Once we were on board, we would throw or slide all of our equipment to the center of the chopper and sit on the edge of the side openings to let our legs hang out over the edge. It was so peaceful and cool. I don't remember anyone that didn't sit on the edge to cool off. If they were afraid of heights, they could sit on one of door edges and hang on to the door frame. All and all, those pickup flights were the happiest times of our missions. We were relaxing, we were looking forward to a cold shower and hot meal, and we were celebrating the survival of another mission. Those were our best times on a slick, going away from the fight. We had had enough for a while and these birds were giving us a short rest.

"One more dance along the razor's edge finished. Almost dead yesterday, maybe dead tomorrow, but alive, gloriously alive, today."

—Robert Jordan, *Lord of Chaos*

CHAPTER 23

LAI KHE

The Area of Operations for us when we worked out of Lai Khe was old established NVA territory. The region was about 30 to 35 kilometers from Saigon and consisted of hundreds of square miles of basecamps used as staging areas for NVA operations into the greater Saigon area. To us these areas were known as the Iron Triangle, the Ho Bo Woods, the Michelin Rubber Plantation, the Trapezoid and other names. These areas were used by various Vietnamese fighting units going all the way back to World War II when the Vietnamese were fighting the Japanese Imperial Army.

The terrain was widely diverse. There were areas of extremely dense jungle, heavy bamboo, lots of rubber trees, semi-open bush lands, a couple of large rivers and a few hills. Now add hundreds of enemy basecamps (most of them abandoned and/ or bombed), tens of thousands of large to huge bomb craters (30 feet deep by 40 feet wide), huge expanses of Agent Orange-defoliated land, thousands of unexploded artillery rounds, hundreds of scorched Napalm areas and an active enemy resupply network. All of these factors made working out of Lai Khe interesting, as well as challenging.

In addition to Lai Khe's infamous real estate, the area was well known for its high concentration of Agent Orange. Maps of the use of Agent Orange reveal that our AOs out of Lai Khe had as high a concentration of Agent Orange as anywhere in South Vietnam. Many parts of the Iron Triangle and other heavily infiltrated areas were desolate landscapes with only bare tree trunks and deep bomb craters. These bleak regions had been defoliated and bombed numerous times over years of enemy contact.

In the dry season, we breathed, ate and were in constant contact with dirt and dust that was saturated with Agent Orange. In the wet season, we had either wet or dried contaminated mud on us continually. Of course this condition would last for two to three weeks until we would return to the basecamp and shower. But then we would go right back out into those field conditions the next morning. When we would sometimes run out of water, out of necessity we would fill our canteens with local (contaminated) water. We were having Dioxin enter our bodies in just about every way that was possible.

The map also shows that heavy Agent Orange was used at every other main AO in which I worked: Quan Loi, Song Be and Dau Tieng. In retrospect, I now realize that I never worked anywhere that was free of Agent Orange.

CHAPTER 24

AN EXAMPLE OF WORKING THE LAI KHE AREA

The best example of working the Lai Khe area as a grunt was an operation during which I recall going into the Trapezoid. We flew into the only open area that could be used for an LZ for miles so we knew that it was likely there would be ground fire as we landed, making it a hot LZ. We flew into an area of tall (4'-6') grasses and we jumped out about three to four feet above the ground and landed in about 12 to 16 inches of bog. Immediately afterwards the two pilots and two door gunners jumped out when their chopper hit the ground; I had felt (heard?) a few rounds hit our chopper, but I didn't realize that a round had hit something important like an oil or hydraulic line.

When you have a downed chopper in a hot LZ, everything changes. The first wave (my group) started running for the tree line to begin securing the area. Our speed was drastically slowed because of the 12" to 16" of muck and soggy grass roots. So we were in the open and vulnerable much longer than normal. The only good news was that we quickly (in about 15 minutes) received a gunship to support us. We got special service since we had that very valuable downed helicopter on the ground.

A couple more waves came in, and things were getting a little easier. We were increasing our numbers and we were experiencing fading enemy fire. Within a couple hours we had the entire

Chinook slinging a downed slick (Courtesy commons.wikipedia.org.)

company and a couple of helicopter mechanics on the ground. But the company now had to secure a much larger area so that a large lift helicopter could fly in and lift out the slick.

So the company began securing a large area around the LZ so that the large, slow lift helicopter could lift and carry the slick back to a repair facility. An area about a kilometer (1 kilometer = .62 miles) around the LZ was required. The company had to send a number of patrols out at least another kilometer in all directions to ensure that the big chopper would be safe.

Basically it took most of the daylight hours to get the valuable asset back home, safe and sound, and for us to finally get ready to begin our mission. With all the time and noise that we made that day, we knew that we were in the middle of one of the tougher spots in our AO. It was certain that every NVA within 50 kilometers knew where we were and how many of us were on the ground. It was decided that instead of setting up ambushes that night, we had better move a few kilometers and find a good spot to dig in (set up a Night Defensive Position or NDP) and wait for what we expected to be a long night.

Sure enough we were probed by the enemy in several places that night, but we were able to use illumination flares at a distance behind the probes in order to direct effective artillery support. The idea of using the back flares was that we didn't want illumination over us because then the enemy could easily see our positions. Also having the illumination behind the enemy silhouetted them well enough that we could see them and bring in the artillery and target them effectively. Naturally, this practice only works in more open areas and not in thick jungle or rubber tree forests.

So we made it through the night and started walking in a straight line all day. It was tough walking because we were going through one B-52 bombed area after another. All day long we walked over or around 500 and 1000 pound bomb craters from one bombing mission after another. Those conditions were very tiring because of all of the hills of loose dirt at the crater's edge and it was literally one crater edge touching the next. As we walked away from the LZ, we went through a succession of one very large basecamp after another. We trudged through eight or ten or twelve of those basecamps—I really can't recall the exact number. Each successive one would be a bit newer than the last bombed-out one. Finally after we walked through a recently bombed-out basecamp, we walked directly into a very large firefight. Guess what? We had walked right into a very large occupied basecamp and all hell broke loose. Of course they knew we were coming because they had been watching us since the day before, so they were ready. We flanked to our right and left and found bunkers, indicating a substantial basecamp, so our fearless leaders decided to fight backwards and to the side (retreat) to try to break contact.

We moved as fast and as far as we could and finally dug in for an NDP. But this night turned out to be an easier night, and we were not harassed as much. We knew that they were abandoning their basecamp because they knew that it was going to be bombed soon. Yup, overnight our battalion called in a

B-52 strike for the next morning. We got up early, moved away a couple of clicks and waited for the air strike. After the strike, we went back to the enemy basecamp and found it destroyed and empty, with no casualties. All of my fellow grunts knew that in five to six months some poor infantry company from the First Division would land into the same hot LZ, march through the same bombed-out terrain, passing all of the same bombed-out basecamps PLUS ONE and then walk into another very dangerous firefight. The grunt casualties didn't seem to matter to the lifers, but to find another B-52 bombing target was great fun for the big boys.

CHAPTER 25

FLASHLIGHTS

Sometimes, when we were working in an active AO, we would set up an ambush, and a few hours into the night, lights from flashlights would appear outside of our perimeter. It was impossible to know if they were regular flashlights at a long distance or smaller pen lights that were much closer to our position. There could be a few or scores or sometimes even a hundred lights. Once they were turned on they would stay on and not move. To this day I don't know anything about them other than they always gave us the creeps. Imagine that you are with 20 to 25 men in ambush and that over a two-hour period, 50 or 100 faint lights are turned on and pointed in your direction. Trust me—it is a very unsettling feeling.

The general consensus among us was that the NVA knew we were in the area but did not know our exact location, so they would use the lights to try to spook us into breaking our silence discipline and thereby reveal our position. The most important rule in being in an ambush was not to allow your exact location to be known. When an ambush is set, the positions are not dug in (you're on top of the ground), so there was no element of an ambush that was defensive (because in a defensive stance, holes are dug). It is an offensive tactic only. When the ambush was popped, we would move to a different position because the existing position was not defendable. So silence is critical to the success of seeing the next dawn. The flashlight nights were always difficult nights to get through.

CHAPTER 26

ANOTHER GREAT IDEA FROM ABOVE

"The journey of a thousand miles begins with one step, and a lot of bitching."
—Unknown

One evening after returning to the basecamp and cleaning up, the CO called a company formation to talk with us—not good, really not good. He told us that the company was going way south out of our AO to help out with patrols along the Saigon River. Our mission was to locate (stumble upon?) rocket-launching sites whose rockets had become bothersome to Saigon City. "Great! We get to have a new learning experience for a four-day operation," we all thought with dread.

The next morning, we were all loaded down with five days of supplies and trucked to the air strip. We waited for a C-130 cargo plane for hours, sitting in full gear in the very hot sun. All three rifle platoons were loaded into the plane (80 to 90 men) along with the company's potable water trailer. Except for this trip I never saw the water trailer when it was anywhere but in the Company Headquarters' yard. Why we hauled it in the plane was a secret never shared with the grunts.

We were all sitting in the plane, cross legged in full gear on the aircraft's flat pallets that moved on a track. We had been hot outside while waiting, and now we were really roasting in the stifling dead air inside the plane. We waited for one and a half or two hours before we took off. Our legs and backs were in agony from the knots and cramps that we were all experiencing. To add to the pain, when the plane finally did move the pallets would slide one or two inches back-and-forth on the track, causing even more stabs of pain in our bodies. No wonder the military wanted young men!

Finally we landed at an air strip, walked over to some choppers and prepared for another aerial insertion. My gun crew loaded up for the first wave and took off. We flew out and soon saw a large river winding through a plain of grass. We landed on a faintly defined road or ridge two or three feet above the grass on firm ground. I do recall that we were not worried about the LZ being "hot" because we could see in all directions and there was nothing out there but us.

So we started to spread out to secure the area and stepped off the path and into a sopping mixture of grass, roots and mud. We were in the middle of a huge tidal marsh and we all sank into the muck up to our crotches—yes, it was really that deep! We had to actually use one arm (the other arm was busy holding up our weapons to keep them dry) to pull our legs out of the mess, over-coming both mud and suction, followed by a step one foot ahead. I don't think any of us moved more than five feet before the next wave came in. The Platoon Leader saw the problem by then and had the rest of the men just spread up and

Alpha Company disembarking from the C130 on our way to the helipads

down the path. We original 20 men just stayed where we were in the muck.

After the entire company was on the ground they spread out on the road for 500 feet or more. The Company Commander (CO) gathered the officers and had a powwow. I think that the 20 of us that were still in the muck had proved the idiocy of this mission within 30 minutes of our landing; if we couldn't move in these conditions then neither could an NVA or Viet Cong missile launching crew. They would be in the open, slow and very vulnerable. But after a conference and a call to Battalion Headquarters the company formed into two columns and plodded forward through the mud heading to nowhere.

I don't think that we traveled 25 to 50 yards that short afternoon before the tide started to rise. The water level started to move up our bodies, and we were still stuck in the mud. It soon got chest deep and still rising. We were all starting to panic and were starting to talk about dropping off all of our gear that was strapped to us and in our pockets. All we could do was hold our weapons above our heads. We were completely combat-ineffective for the next three days. All of our ammo, many weapons and even our weapon-cleaning gear were fouled with both mud and salt water. With the water level higher, we noticed patches of taller grass, and that night we all tried to get to those areas so that we could bend them over and get our feet out of the muck and "float," getting part of our bodies out of the water for a portion of the night.

The only thing wrong with these "tall grass islands" that we built was that some of them had the dreaded RED ANTS in the grass. These ants were one of the worst adversaries faced by the infantry. One or two of the groups of men actually abandoned their "islands" because of these monsters. These groups would in fact rather slog through the muck chest to neck deep in water than share the space with the red ants. In fact, my own machine gun crew moved eventually.

This entire area was all grass except for a network of creeks or streams that would distribute the water into or out of the grass as the tide came in or out. These became quite a dangerous problem because when we crossed them with the tide in, they were deep enough to drown us. When the tide was out they were deep, slimy and slippery ditches that were almost impossible to climb out of and then we would be totally covered with mud until the tide came back in. Plus when the tide was coming in or going out, these rivulets became torrents of water that would sweep us away if we were not tethered to a secured line while crossing them.

The morning after our first night there we started slogging our way in some direction, and we looked across the tops of the grass and saw an ocean-going ship about a half mile away. What a shock! It was effortlessly sliding through the grass just as easily as can be. The river we all saw as we came in was the main shipping lane, and this freighter was heading up river to Saigon to offload its cargo—and there we were in our four-day hell. As time passed, we probably saw six or seven ships on the river.

We spent two more nights and three more days moving and becoming absolutely exhausted. We finally made it to the river and got picked up by a Navy landing craft. On our trip back to some Navy facility, the sailors broke out hoses for us, and we spent most of the couple-hour trip hosing each other down with river water. We hosed down ourselves as well as our weapons and cleaning kits. We were totally spent as we started cleaning our weapons. This whole operation was so dangerous for us, yet it had NO military value. We were essentially combat-ineffective for the whole time we were on the ground (in the muck), and we saw not a single sign of any enemy activity. No human being could have used that area for any kind of activity.

CHAPTER 27

A VISIT TO THE POST EXCHANGE (PX)

When we were back in basecamp it was easy to identify the infantry. We had the most faded green fatigues, often with few or missing patches and many with small or patched holes. We were the only soldiers wearing steel pots in the basecamps because we didn't even have a hat to put on heads. Our steel pot cloth covers and our boots were stained a permanent red from the red soil of our area. Everyone looked semi-stateside, with their shined boots and tricked out uniforms but us. We were the faded and dusty hand-me-down grunts.

I remember a day when I had probably been in-country two or three months when our entire company was given the opportunity to go to the PX.. Wow, what a treat. Going to the PX was almost like being a civilian for an hour. The PX was a department store for the REMFs and we had never had time to go.

As we finished our assignments, we trickled over to the PX. Many of us had never been in it and were pretty excited to get a chance to be there. Anyone stationed in Lai Khe except the infantry could go to the PX any number of times a week. Anyway, there was either a stupid or a new Military Policemen (MP) posted at the PX who was not allowing anyone from our company into the PX because we did not have proper uniforms. Of course we had clean, newly issued fatigues with no name or unit or other proper patches on them because we were wearing our uniforms issued from our 90th replacement castaway uniforms.

Predictably things quickly went to hell as we were not about to have our precious time in the PX squandered by a PFC (private first class) MP. Wisely, someone (my guess is a PX person) called the MP's CO and our CO before the MP got hurt. We had simply picked him up and thrown him aside. I guess he got huffy and was trying to reach for his side arm. Our Captain quite publicly told the MP Captain to get his PFC the hell out of our way because we were going into the PX (many of the A ½ men were already inside). It is the only time that I ever witnessed one officer loudly yelling at another.

Two points can be made over that incident; one is that our CO had to stick up for us. We were tired, dangerous and primed to be in the PX since we were never allowed in it. We knew some punk MP kid was not going to stop us because of our issued uniforms. The second point is that he had to be "our man" and fight for us. I do recall that our faith and support for him was greatly increased and that our morale after "the PX incident" (as it came to be known) was greatly improved for a time. I now look back and find that whole episode quite pathetic.

CHAPTER 28

BAD WATER

Most men carried four or five quarts of water, using a combination of one-quart, hard plastic canteens and two-quart, soft sided (and moderately easy to puncture) plastic bladders. It was not uncommon for us to run out of drinking water before we were resupplied in the field, so we were all issued a small bottle of iodine pills that were supposed to disinfect any water we used in the field. Many of us would not carry them to save weight and refused to use them (if we got infected, a few days on sick call or at the hospital would not be all bad, we reasoned).

We were all very disciplined in our personal water usage so we didn't drink a lot of our water from the local streams; however, one evening I ran out of water. We were going to get resupplied the next day and I tried to make it, but I needed water. So I filled my canteen with water from a stream. When one of the point men saw me fill up, he told me that there was a small village upstream. He knew there was a village there because he had a map (I never saw any of the few maps in the platoon). Usually we wouldn't drink that water because the village used it for sanitation and livestock purposes, and we would choose to use a different source for our drinking water.

However, there would be no other supply for me that night, so I kept that water. We were all kept busy for the rest of the hour by moving into our ambush site and setting it up. It was now totally dark. A few minutes after settling in, I decided to sanitize this very suspect water. The disinfecting water process was new to Jimmy and me since we had never tried to clean any water before. In fact neither of us had the required iodine tablets with us. So I checked with our ammo bearer and of course he had his; he was too new to have figured out which things could be thrown away.

There were parts of this process that were going to present a problem. How many tablets were required for a quart of water and should I crush the tabs or would they dissolve in the water. It had been months since either Jimmy or I had read the directions on the label. When a person is first out in the field, he reads everything he can. Every label on every can, every article of clothing and every piece of equipment is read multiple times. It helps the endless time pass, but by week two there is nothing new left to read.

So I asked our new ammo bearer about these facts; he told me that I needed two to four tablets per quart, so I put in eight because I knew this water was foul. (I am completely making up these amounts because I really don't remember them.) He told me that he couldn't remember if we were supposed to crush them so I did. I shook it well for a few minutes and thought, "That ought to do it." It was terrible tasting, but I took a drink. We all forgot that the directions state that the water should stand for at least one half hour for the disinfectant to work.

In the night I really got some bad cramps and the symptoms of diarrhea. I couldn't take a crap because of the noise and smell; either would give away our position. *Finally* dawn came, and I crawled away to relieve myself. I crawled back and I could scarcely move. Doc Bernardini (Mike Platoon's medic) came over and gave me something, and somehow I moved out with the platoon.

Doc Pete Bernardini

The day was a resupply day, and I couldn't have cared less, because I was so sick. I finally got to our LZ position and just curled into a fetal position. The other Mike Platoon machine gunner (Assistant Squad Leader) organized the men to get the C rations, mail, clean clothes and other things for the platoon instead of me.

My doc (Pete Bernardini) wanted to send me back with the supply ships so that I could report to sick call, but our asshole First Sergeant would have nothing to do with it. I can still clearly see Doc and Top (First Sergeant) literally nose-to-nose and with fingertips to each other's chests screaming at each other. Minion Doc was standing up to the most powerful lifer in our company and very publicly shouting, "I'll have your stripes for this, Top!"

Everybody within earshot dropped their jaws in disbelief. Doc had just publicly challenged Top's authority. Top! To the grunts he was the most powerful person in the company. He truly held our lives in the palm of his hand. He and his Army network could arrange to send any one of us on an assignment where there would be no return. And Doc had just publicly double-dog dared him into a situation where one or the other would be the winner within half an hour. If I was returned to basecamp, then Doc had bettered Top's authority; if I stayed with the company and continued to suffer, then Doc's bluff was called, and Doc would have to bring formal charges against Top.

Technically, a final medical decision in the field was to be the Medic's call. On the other hand, in a military court, a draftee

Loach helicopters were usually used for scouting (Courtesy www.militaryfactory.com)

would very seldom win against a lifer. However, it would also be bad for Top's record. Finally they split up and went their own ways, and the resupply operation continued and then finished as the last choppers flew away. Shit, Top had won.

Soon Lima and November platoons split away and started their separate patrols for the day. For some reason Mike Platoon stayed behind and made a smaller LZ. In a few minutes, Doc came up to me and told me to follow him. So I gave my M60 to Jimmy and took Jimmy's M16.

I went to the center of the LZ and asked Doc what was up. He told me that Top had radioed for a passing Loach, which was the Battalion Commander's chopper, to pick me up and drop me off at base for sick call. So I went. The company still believed that I did not go back to go to sick call, so Top had saved face in front of the rest of the company, for now.

By the time I got to camp, sick call had been over for an hour, and I never did see a doctor. No help, no record and back on-line the next day. Just for the record, twenty years later I had to have my entire ulcerated colon removed.

CHAPTER 29

DOG TAGS

From the grunts' viewpoint, working out of Lai Khe in these old and established areas was a bit of a crap shoot. This AO was part of the Ho Chi Minh trail system but also an area of troop and material storage where there were multiple enemy basecamps. After the first day, we would work in platoon-sized patrols (25-30 men) and ambushes. Usually our contacts during the daylight hours would involve bumping into four to eight enemies humping material on a trail. The firefight would be quick and perhaps fierce but would be over quickly; moreover, they would rapidly disappear because they didn't want to sustain contact. However, every once in a while, the platoon would stumble into a hefty basecamp. A firefight would quickly ensue, and the platoon would be very much outnumbered. At this point, we called in air support (mostly helicopter gunships) and artillery and hoped like hell that we could break contact or that the other two platoons of our company could come to aid us if we needed help. When we were in heavy contact we would sometimes call in air support and get some F-4 Phantom jets with bombs and napalm to help us out. That was life in the Big Red One.

Each time we made our one-night turn-around in our basecamp (once every two or three weeks), the Squad leaders would perform an inspection of each man to make sure that each person had everything that was required in the field. If we had returned to base after a significant firefight, then the Platoon Leader, instead of the squad leader, would inspect each man. If we heard that the upcoming mission was going to be a "bad" one, then some of the old timers would say that they had lost their "dog tags" because there was an army regulation that all combatants had to have the tags to go into the field. So these sneaky strategists would be on the list for new tags. Yet in spite of the regulation, every one of our butts (sans tags) would be on the choppers flying out to the LZ anyway. Usually the tags were backlogged from supply and then later many orders would be filled at once. On one turnaround, I was issued four sets of dog tags—finally catching up!

Soldiers had two schools of thought about dog tags. One group of men would never be without their tags. The very thought of their bodies being lost or not identified was one of their biggest fears. Then there was the school of thought to which I subscribed. If there was a one-in-a-million chance that someone was going to yank me off that chopper because I didn't have my tags, then I was going to take those odds and throw away my tags. If I wasn't on that chopper, then I couldn't get shot. If I was in the bush without my tags and did get shot, then some rear echelon fucker could do the extra work to sort out my identification mess. It was no skin off my nose.

* * *

Working in the Lai Khe AO was often somewhat boring; however, our patrol could also turn into an extremely heavy firefight on the turn of a dime. It made no difference what area our mission would take us; the enemy would always be present. I always hated working out of Lai Khe.

PART 5

QUAN LOI

CHAPTER 30

QUAN LOI

Sometime later my Brigade of the 1st Division moved its headquarters north from Lai Khe up Highway 13 to Quan Loi. It was also very near some other famous real estate, the towns of An Loc, Loc Ninh and Quan Loi. These villages were located on or near the northern end of Highway 13 and were about 15-25 kilometers from the Cambodian border. This territory was near the beginning of the branches of the Ho Chi Mihn trail that brought supplies down toward Saigon—in other words, we were upstream on the same trails that were near Lai Khe.

The Lai Khe AO was challenging because of the old established enemy supply caches, basecamps and infrastructure, but the Quan Loi AO had a long tradition of political support for the enemy. Loc Ninh was North Vietnam's Provisional Capital City for the south. The popular support for the North Vietnamese in the area was unwavering and long-established, probably going back to French Colonial times.

In the 1930's, there were several labor strikes by plantation workers against Michelin Rubber in the area, and during one extended strike, the local plantation manager invited the Quan Loi worker's leaders to his mansion where they were apprehended and then taken to the beautiful colonial town square in An Loc. There they were disemboweled, beheaded and left hanging in the town square. So here too we had our troubles.

Quan Loi was the largest basecamp that I ever worked out of. It was also the northernmost basecamp of the 1st Infantry Division. Inside its wire were a long airstrip (3900'), 10-15 helicopters, and a large collection of the biggest artillery assigned to the first division. These artillery pieces included 105s, 155s, 175s, and 8"s. These were big guns and they needed a lot of security. There were also scores of semi-permanent army buildings used for the entire Brigade's administration and each of the battalions' administrations. In addition to our five Infantry Battalions, our brigade also had the 11th Armored Cavalry attached to it. Over a thousand soldiers were permanently based there, in addition to several thousand who moved back and forth between the basecamp and the field. My very dubious estimate is that the basecamp was one and a half to two miles long by three quarters of a mile to one mile wide.

Modern Cavalry units (since WWI) are ground troops with special inherent advantages in combat such as mechanized transportation (like tanks and tracks) or air-mobility. These advantages were as important as the horse was to earlier cavalry units. Although the 1st Division had some mechanized units in it, the entire Division had integral air assets and operated as an air-mobile force.

CHAPTER 31

WORKING INSIDE THE WIRE

Some of my most memorable times were at Quan Loi. I have several funny memories as well as the memory of my worst nights spent in-country. First, on most nights the basecamp did not have combat troops inside the wire for defense. The bunkers for the base were manned by cooks, clerk typists, mechanics and all sorts of other rear-echelon personnel. Usually the combat troops were out in the field. If we were in overnight we would arrive late in the afternoon and fly out at dawn the next day. But twice, for some unknown reason to us grunts, our company was brought into the basecamp for three days of bunker duty. Almost all of my photos of Mike Platoon were taken during these wonderful and lazy days. It was heaven!

Our Company was spread out on a single stretch of the bunker line and assigned three men to a bunker. Since senior NCOs and Officers were not in the bunkers, I suppose our company took up about 20 to 23 bunkers out of several hundred. Of course my bunker mates were my assistant gunner and our ammo bearer. Remember, you never mess with the gun crew. The rest of the bunkers were occupied by guys from the same squads, so everyone was in bunkers with their friends.

Mail would be delivered to us in the field every resupply day but only the letters. Packages were given to us only when we were inside the wire. So usually we would get multiple packages and have one late afternoon and evening to eat it all. The

Jim Gray smoking and reading mail in the shade on the Quan Loi bunker line.

unwritten rule was everyone shared the cookies, cakes, bars and all of the fresh stuff but kept the sardines, kipper snacks, Vienna Sausages and other canned treats for themselves in the field as a change from the C rations that we usually had. The result was that much of the fresh food our mothers, sisters, wives and girlfriends sent were thrown away because the army wouldn't give us time to eat it. Everyone else in the army had time but not the draft infantry.

But life was great when we were on bunker duty in Quan Loi. We had multiple days to relax, and we actually had time to enjoy our care packages. We weren't humping our gear, or drenched in stinking clothes, or spending all day and night extremely thirsty, or on edge for long stretches of time. We were clean, well hydrated and relaxed. And best of all, we got two or three hot meals a day. Our battalion mess would cook

Hanging out on the Quan Loi bunker line.

something hot and bring it out to the bunker line and serve us there. For those few days, life was great!

During those days on the basecamp's bunker line, we usually had some small assignments to do in the mornings but we would have most of the afternoon to ourselves. I usually "volunteered" my squad to burn shit from the outhouses. In the outhouses the shit was collected in large pans made from cut-down fifty five gallon drums. So daily someone would grab a large hook and drag the pans out from the back of the outhouse, add diesel fuel and "burn the shit." At first my men were pissed at me about it but soon figured out that it was the easiest and "quickest" of all the duties. All one needed to do was pull out the shit cans, pour in and light the fuel, do a quick cleaning of the inside and then just sit back, up-wind of course, and relax. It was easy to stretch it out three or more hours; after all, who was going to check on us? We burned a lot of fuel with no shit in it. Then in the afternoons we could nap on and off, write letters, perhaps play some taped music, play cribbage and nap some more.

At night we would pull our guard rotation between the three of us, but it was easy to do behind the wire. For one reason, it was much lighter in the open instead of under the dark canopy of jungle, rubber trees or bamboo. If the moon was out, we could often write letters home. We also slept better on the board bunks than on the uneven, lumpy and often wet ground out in the field.

I remember one night on bunker duty we received our usual incoming rockets and mortars when all of a sudden there was one huge secondary explosion. KAPOW!! Then all sorts of other smaller explosions followed and then continued. What the Hell? We knew the enemy hit something good but what was it? Soon the news came over our company radio that the enemy had hit the main artillery ammo dump in the basecamp. The fireworks went on all night.

Our battalion Head Quarters Company was the company with all of our rear echelon clerks, cooks, officers and also a special weapons platoon. Assigned to this platoon were two 4.2" (large) mortars with crews, a Jeep mounted 106mm recoilless rifle and some other various large weapons that did not go into the field because of the local terrain and cover from the vegetation. The recoilless was manned by guys that had been grunts in the field and who had been good, reliable soldiers, usually point men, radio operators (RTOs) or machine gunners. So they had been rewarded by the battalion by being pulled off line and given this safer job inside the wire.

Their job was to remain proficient using and maintaining the 106mm recoilless during the day. At night, they would drive the recoilless into a permanent position between our bunker and the next bunker and spend the night talking, smoking pot and sleeping. They were sleeping well because they knew that they had Company A's grunts in their bunker sector and that we would be awake and diligent in our guard duty.

Just before dark each position on the bunker line would pull the pins and wedge trip flares into the inside-most coils of wire out in front of the bunkers. This was done so that if the coils were disturbed (in theory by an enemy penetration) the flares would be dislodged, fall to the ground and light up the area that was disturbed. In the mornings, we would retrieve them and put the pin back in. However, the 106 crew was lazy and just left theirs in the wire all of the time so that they wouldn't waste their time installing or retrieving them. So one afternoon we took one of our flares and put it in the wire in front of them and made a very long trip wire that led over to our bunker. We

Bogie inserting trip flares in the wire just before sundown.

then passed the word to all of Company A's bunkers about what we had done.

At sundown, the 106 crew arrived right on time and started their normal routine. At around 2:00 a.m. we pulled the trip wire from our bunker, and the flare fell and fired up. All of the men in the nearby Alpha Company bunkers were howling with laughter as we watched the slightly stoned 106 crew wake up and run around in panic. Great sadistic fun was played by infantry grunts on any available rear echelon soldier, even former grunts.

* * *

I recall one evening meal when we were in Quan Loi for a resupply overnight. For some reason our Company was standing in chow line at a mess hall other than our battalion's. It was located next to the airstrip. As we were waiting, some incoming mortar or rockets started to drop in on the airstrip. They were a couple of hundred yards away from us and the rounds were "walking" up the airstrip towards us. They were not threatening us so we just stayed put and watched the rounds "walk" towards some parked helicopters. That day the enemy got lucky, and one round hit a helicopter and blew it up along with the top half of the choppers on each side. The incoming stopped, and we stayed in line and just watched the two damaged choppers burn, not giving much thought to them.

All of a sudden there was a gigantic explosion as one of the damaged choppers blew up. It was much more powerful than the original direct hit. About one second later, the entire chow line was knocked on our butts as if a giant air pillow had been slammed into us. I don't understand why the second explosion was stronger unless it was fuel or ordinance-related, but we recovered, laughed and continued to wait for our hot meal.

CHAPTER 32

QUAN LOI MISSIONS

The Quan Loi AO had many, many square miles of rubber plantations, and we spent many operations in them. Rubber tree farms had thousands of 30' to 40' trees planted in a 15' x 15' grid. Rubber trees were planted on flat ground and hilly ground. Below is a picture of a farm that is actively being tapped. The ground between the rows is covered with low and maintained ground cover.

Oftentimes we would see plantation workers in the farm performing their tasks during the day. In fact, if we were on patrol in a farm that was being worked and we did not see workers,

Rubber forest (Courtesy commons.wikipedia.org.)

we would oftentimes be a little bit more alert because often they would disappear if they knew that some enemy troops were nearby.

We also had operations in rubber farms that were not being tapped where the undergrowth was six to eight feet high and mildly dense. At night, no matter how bright the moon it would be too dark in a rubber plantation for our one crude Starlight Scope (early night vision) to work effectively.

In one operation I recall, we had a new company commander. I recall how he was always in a hurry and was always trying new ideas in the field without thinking through the undesired consequences of the change. We had just been inserted and were moving away from the LZ for a couple clicks in "company formation." In company formation, all three platoons moved in two columns with one platoon behind the other. We were patrolling working rubber so the undergrowth was clean and short with good visibility in all directions.

Normally the columns would walk with one or two rows of trees between them and off center in the spaces so that a row of trees was close to the outside of the formation. This allowed a tree to be an immediate and readymade cover behind which to step during the first moments of a firefight. However, on this day, the idiot Company Commander decided that in this open rubber he wanted more firepower up front. So he dreamed up a formation in which I, the machine gunner, was the point man and was walking down the center of the space between two rows of trees; then five paces behind and four to five feet to each side were my assistant gunner and my ammo bearer. Next, five paces behind and about four or five feet out were finally two men from the point squad. Two more men from the point squad were five paces back and again four feet out from the men forward of them. The columns were then formed behind these last men. In other words, the front of the two columns was an inverted "V" formed by the machine gun crew.

Let's critique this idiocy. First, an important rule of the infantry is not to mess with the safety of the machine gun. The gun needs to be protected and centrally located so that it can be placed into action as soon as possible. This new formation placed the gun in the most vulnerable location possible and it was definitely not centrally-located. Ordinarily the men of the point squad, having been individually trained and with keen senses for spotting suspicious and dangerous signs ahead of the formation, are placed in the very front of the platoon so those skills are used effectively. However, with this formation, they were placed at least ten paces (15' to 20') behind the actual point. Instead of having these specialists out front, the three men that were carrying the most important weapon and the most weight in the company were out front, slogging through the countryside as perfect targets.

With this configuration, as the V is formed, the men in the two columns are laterally further and further from each other. The men in the two columns were walking just on the outside of two rows of trees or about 30' apart. In this fairly open terrain the columns were too close together and they had the trees on the wrong side of them for cover. Plus there were seven men making a trail rather than the normal two so that we had a much better chance of tripping a booby trap or mine with this arrangement. The CO's great idea exposed our major firepower, had us bunched up in open terrain, exposed seven people to booby traps and proved to us he was an idiot and would unquestionably get some of us killed needlessly, which indeed he did within a few weeks. He soon had a bounty on his head from his own men.

We continued using this formation for the rest of the day but thankfully never had an incident. We later broke up into platoon formations and went to set up platoon ambushes that night. Man, was I glad to leave the CO with one of the other platoons.

Our CO continued to be an idiot in the field for some time. He cost us a number of casualties from his eagerness and stupidity. There was complete consensus among the grunts during my tenure that he was the worst CO of the three that we had during that year. Later he was relieved from his command and taken out of the field by the Battalion CO, and we never heard from him again. We all hoped he never got another command.

* * *

Another mission was to guard a critical bridge in the huge Michelin Rubber forest. This bridge had a continuous security detail, and we were just one company of many that would rotate into this mission.

There were permanent fighting positions (fox holes) all around the bridge with the command post on one bank. On the opposite side of the stream and a bit removed was a village that sat up at a slightly higher elevation. In the village was some sort of a primitive rubber processing plant in several large metal buildings.

This was not an ideal military situation. First, the village was NOT a free-fire zone. So it was difficult to defend the bridge from attacks on that side of the river because the fire restrictions in the village limited our reactions. Therefore, close support such as gunships, artillery and air strikes were hampered. Second, the village would allow an enemy force to get very close and have the advantage of high ground over our defenses before they would attack. Third, there was also the threat of submerged sappers breathing through straws floating down the river to the bridge.

Even with those threats, the duty there seemed easy for us. For some reason, even though the bridge was used by the US military, it did not seem to be a priority target for the NVA. As a result, we had three days of lying around, napping, reading and writing letters and hydrating.

The part of that mission that I remember the most is the sapper defense component. About ten feet below the deck of the bridge was a narrow catwalk. Three or four times an hour this was used by a soldier to discourage submerged enemy fighters by dropping grenades into the river. Next to the catwalk was a case of MK3A2 concussion grenades. These were water proof grenades that when exploded produced enormous pressure waves that would severely wound any underwater combatant near the bridge. To further confuse the threats, there was an intentional effort to not have a predictable time pattern in the use of the grenades.

One consequence of our strategy was that in late mornings and afternoons we would often see a few villagers gather below the bridge 20 or 30 meters and wait for our blasting. The blast would always stun a few fish which were nearby, which would cause them to rise to the surface and float downstream to the villagers. There were never a large number of fish caught because it would only be about 15 or 20 minutes since the last explosion, but there were always a few. My guess was that there were probably a greater number of fish meals in that village than in most other inland villages.

* * *

As I recall now, there seemed to be a large number of aerial insertions that had something memorable about them. A number of them were hot and things could always have gone better for those. But many of the cool LZs (with no enemy fire power) had their own problems. Once we came into an LZ with beautiful swaying grass about four feet tall. "Ah," I thought, "this will be a nice soft landing" as I jumped off of the chopper from about four feet off the ground. Little did I know that the grass was growing in about a foot of water with a mucky root system. My feet and everybody else's went straight through the grass and root system until we were about three feet into the water and muck. Our feet were spread wider than our shoulders, and many of our old hand-me-down pants split from our back belt loops to the bottom of our fly opening. Since no one wore underwear in the field because of chafing, the men of good ol' Mike platoon were "hangin' free" for the next several days until our next resupply. Yes, there were a number of events that related to our "costume failure" over the next few days, involving a variety of plants and animals. After a long discussion, Mike platoon decided to radio the following platoons to warn them about the situation and spare them the fate that we had to suffer. Their gratitude did not keep them from laughing and teasing us for a few weeks.

* * *

Early one morning at Quan Loi, I remember waiting for our choppers to pick us up for an insertion into the field. Mike Platoon was to be the first wave, so we were upset when only three choppers came in to pick us all up—damn. The insertion was going to be located in a hairy location, so it was decided to break our rules and load the first chopper with my gun crew and the Platoon Sergeant with his radioman, because we wanted to get as many men as we could on the ground at the LZ. So we were flying two choppers with six men and a very overloaded one with a gun and radio aboard. In addition, it was the first flight of the day for the chopper so the choppers had lots of fuel onboard. We struggled to get off the ground, and soon the pilot tilted his nose down and started to fly forward. When a chopper is very heavy they need to fly forward to increase their lift and therefore their altitude. The chopper was struggling but we were going to get on our way.

We flew for some time, and then we got a wave from a door gunner that meant we were about a minute out of the LZ. That "minute out" signal caused everyone to move to the door openings (recall that all of our Division's choppers had the large cargo doors removed) and step out onto the chopper's skid, holding on to the front or back door frame. We always rode the last mile into the LZ standing on the skid in preparation of jumping off the skid before it ever touched the ground. Since standing on the skid safely required holding on to a door jamb, only four of the five men in our chopper were on the skid. On this flight my friend Mike Humlicek, who was humping the heavy radio for the Platoon Sergeant, was the man that didn't get on the skid ahead of time. So he was sitting in the middle of the chopper floor waiting to jump out either side when it was time to jump out.

The clearing that was our LZ was short in length and had a sharp uphill angle orientation as we came in. Both of these conditions were problematic for our overloaded chopper because we needed to keep our forward speed for the lift. As we descended, the four men on the skids were getting ready to jump off the skid, which usually happened three to four feet off the ground, and run to the tree line as fast as possible. At about eight feet above the ground all of us could feel that the chopper was not going to descend anymore and we all jumped simultaneously. Mike Humlicek also felt the moment and slid to the edge of the floor and pushed off.

What none of us had thought about was that as soon as the four of us jumped, the chopper had much more lift and sprang up as though it was attached to a bungee cord. By the time Mike cleared the chopper floor and had committed to the jump, he was probably 20+ feet above the ground. Jimmy White and I were on the ground about eight or ten feet apart when we

Mike Humlicek at a much happier time.

heard a yell/scream from above us and between us. We both looked up and saw a spread eagled, flailing Mike Humlicek falling and flapping between us. It was well into the dry season and the ground was like an asphalt lot and he hit that unforgiving ground like a concrete block. Every indestructible plastic part on his M16 shattered and the PRC-25 radio strapped to his back drove every cubic millimeter of air out of his lungs. He couldn't move and he couldn't breathe; he was dazed and absolutely done. He was spread-eagled on his stomach with his smashed M16 about four feet from his right fingertips. About a millisecond after the splash and without a word spoken between us, Jimmy grabbed Mike's M16 and one armpit and I grabbed his other armpit and we started to run towards the brush line, dragging Mike's legs and feet behind us. I can't even remember if the LZ was hot or not; we just knew that we were not going to leave Mike and his radio out there in the open.

What we did not think about was that during the dry season the grass and small bush stubble in the clearing was dried out, rigid and sharp. All we thought about was getting him to relative safety, but what we were also doing was shredding his pants and legs as we drug him over that rigid stubble. We just dropped him at the bush line and Jimmy and I focused on the perimeter security.

Sometime later, Mike had eventually pulled himself up so that his back was against a bush or tree, and he was trying to clear his mind and catch his breath. After a few minutes when we finally turned around to check on him, we found an exhausted, bloodied wreck of a man. Jimmy and I couldn't keep from laughing; we had a flashback of his free fall and splash and now could see him as crumpled, ragged mess. Of course that only caused Mike to become infuriated. Eventually he was able to breathe a little bit, and as soon as he could, he hissed at Jimmy and me, "I'll get you two for this, you bastards."

CHAPTER 33

THE ROME PLOW

Another interesting activity with which I became familiar at Quan Loi was the army's use of the Rome Plow. The Rome Plow (made in Rome, NY) was a huge, heavily beefed-up bulldozer that was a cross between a bulldozer and tank. This was the first area in which I saw a Rome Plow and saw the results of using them. Highway 13 went north from Saigon, through the Quan Loi area and beyond to the Cambodian border. There was a short spur road that went from the highway to the Quan Loi basecamp. Both of these roads in this area were cut through dense jungle and brush.

Rome Plow (Courtesy en.wikipedia.org.)

Most of the supplies for the Quan Loi basecamp were brought in by armed convoys. The dense vegetation allowed the enemy to set up convoy ambushes very close to the roads and also aided them with quick and safe withdrawals after the ambush.

The Rome Plows were brought in to clear-cut an area 100 yards on each side of the two roads. This action had a very negative impact on the effectiveness of the enemy ambushes. The enemy ambushes were now forced to be placed 100 yards away which reduced the accuracy and ferocity of the attack.

While the Rome Plows were clearing an area, they needed security both day and night. So usually there was an assigned armored infantry or cavalry unit with them. I remember once spending one or two days pulling security duty for the Plows. We were probably filling in while a couple of other units were rotating in and out. It was pretty easy duty comparatively, with no humping, lots of down time to read and write letters and the opportunity to cat nap all day. What a luxury!

CHAPTER 34

A WELCOME SALUTE

One day we were in basecamp and getting ready for a new operation. We got up early, were fed a quick hot breakfast and loaded into trucks. The trucks took off and drove down the main road in camp and right PAST the airstrip. Oh shit, now what? It was just after daybreak, and they took us to the front gate where the MPs were waiting to open the gates and pull the barriers for us. We offloaded the trucks and with Lima platoon in the lead, the company walked out of the basecamp.

The road was Rome Plowed so we felt fairly secure, and we walked on down the road. In the open like that, I imagine we were eight or ten paces (20' to 25') apart and walking on the outside edges of a two-lane asphalt road. We were stretched out a bit less than 1000' as we started out on what would be a five or six click hike. We had walked a couple of clicks when we heard an airplane fly over to our area, but we didn't think much about it.

All of a sudden we heard a roar behind us, and we realized that that plane was flying wide open and about 15' over our heads. He started from the rear of our columns and flew right past us to a half mile in front of us and just stood the plane on its tail. He climbed up and up and then he cut his engines and stalled the plane. It started coming down tail first when he flipped the nose down, gave it full throttle and leveled out about 20' above the road. He then flew right over our heads again but going from our front to our rear. His turbine engines were just screaming as he pulled up and turned towards the direction of

OV-10A Bronco (Courtesy commons.wikipedia.org.)

his original flight. He gave us a victory roll and disappeared. What a show! I later found out that I just had seen my first OV-10A Bronco. They were very nimble spotter planes used by the Air Force to get right down among the leaves and look under the cover to spot the enemy and mark their location for an air strike. We had just been given a big salute, and he was showing off to the grunts.

We then continued down the road another two or three clicks, made a right angle and walked into the jungle. We never did get an explanation for having to hump to our operation territory, but ignoring the grunts was not a new occurrence. Back into the bush we went.

CHAPTER 35

LIFER PLANNING AT ITS BEST

The only other time that we started an operation through the front gate was again out of Quan Loi, and the operation was one I will never forget. It was the worst night I ever had while suffering no casualties.

First, somewhere in the lifer world they received "intelligence" that a certain village was going to be overflowing with boogie guys, and they came up with a fantastic idea to capture or kill them. Oh boy, here we go!

The plan was for two companies of mechanized infantry, one company from our sister battalion the 2/2 and another company from another unit, to move and block two opposite sides of a village just before daylight, thereby blocking enemy flight in those directions. They were operating close by in the area and could move over in less than an hour. We were to get to our ambush positions on some trails to the south and a click or so from the village. But we had to walk about five clicks to get there. Now there was the rub.

We had to walk through five clicks of hilly rubber at night in absolute darkness. The hills were steep enough that there was a type of terracing there to slow or stop soil erosion. A hole 10 feet wide x 3 feet deep x 3 feet long had been dug between each tree. All of the dirt from the hole was placed immediately next to the hole on the downhill side. The rows of trees with the holes dug between were, of course, the rows that were parallel with the slopes of the hills in order to stop the erosion down the slopes. Each hole was centered between the trees of those parallel rows.

The operation was started the night before with us receiving our normal supplies which were to last four to five days in the field until our first resupply day. So we would be carrying the maximum in weight. Then that evening we were told to go to sleep early because our operation would start at 10:00 p.m. Oh no, this was not good! We were awakened at a few minutes before 10:00 (as if anyone had slept) and were told to put on our gear. Then each platoon was assembled and we were briefed about the night operation. We were next given a small piece of tape about ¾ inch x 1½ inches and told to hold on to it until later. "O.K., five clicks in total dark; we can do this," we all thought.

The trucks showed up at 10:30, and we got in and started towards the front gate. Total silence was emphasized to us over and over, like we needed that reminder. We were unloaded and then assembled into company formation on the road in the basecamp. We were then told to take the tape and affix it, centered and high, on the back of the soldier in front of us in the column. It was florescent tape and we were to follow that glow no matter what, all night long. We were told, "Don't get separated. There won't be any talking to catch up tonight." The MPs opened the gates very quietly and started separating the barbed wire barricades in front of the gates when a trip flare fell out of a barricade onto the road and lit up the whole area. So much for stealth!

So off we went, out the gate, fully loaded and under the bright light of the MPs' sendoff. The usual superstitions of every infantryman kicked in and we all knew that the little flare event was not a good omen. We walked down the road for a few minutes, made an abrupt turn, and into the bush we went. We walked a few more minutes and then we were into rubber and absolute darkness. So far the tape was working OK.

Then we heard the point men falling, slipping and grunting. All of a sudden the tape in front of me went haywire, and then it went down with a clatter. I thought, "Oh, shit," just as I stumbled, fell and kept sliding until I rammed into the guy in front of me at the bottom of a hole. We soon knew what was happening because we had patrolled through an area of rubber with these same terraces a couple of weeks earlier. Oh, my God, we were going to walk all night through this hell. Instantly we all knew there was no way we were going to quietly make the next four clicks before daybreak, and we were right. Somehow through sheer determination, we made it to our objective near the village by daybreak. However, there was no way that 75 men could maintain silence while tripping, sliding, falling and grunting. It was a horrid night. We were totally blind, defenseless to any kind of enemy action, barely functioning as a combat unit and loud as hell. We stopped short of the village in time, but we surely were not stealthy for most of our trip. I'm sure the villagers were fully awake by the time both our company, and the very noisy mechanized companies arrived at our respective points.

The third mechanized unit arrived a few minutes after the first two and thunderously swept through the village to frighten the enemy into running out of the village to the south and into our blazing guns. We knew that every villager knew of our presence as well as the mechanized units and no one was about to move towards us.

What a farce. Our forces roared in and . . . nothing. Where do I begin? First, if the big boys wanted us stealthily to walk five clicks in the dark, then someone should have scouted our route to make sure that we could actually cover those five clicks effectively. If it was discovered to be thick jungle or marshes, they would not have expected us to make that distance. They should have known that it was not possible to accomplish our mission in that treacherous terrain with any kind of silence or safety. Second, if they wanted us to hump silently, then someone in the chain of command should have decided to not make us hump our heaviest loads. We could have carried light and then, after this mission, we could have been resupplied in the field. Or, after the mission they could have even sent us back to Quan Loi to load up for the next mission. Instead we were loaded down with our normal 5 days of canned C-Rations and water, adding weight and noise to our difficult mission.

Finally, why did they think that they could sneak armored units silently or quickly enough to trap the enemy in his own home area? And why did they trust their often faulty intelligence?

This was another example of a stupid, dangerous mission based on faulty intelligence, planned without a single thought about the workings of the soldiers and with no results, other than to simmer in us a more intense hatred for the lifers in our army.

That walk was so difficult because it was done in total darkness. The night vision the soldiers use now is a fantastic additional tool for the modern soldier. It is light weight, compact, dependable, rugged and very effective. We carried the first generation of night vision, and it was just more weight to carry. It was heavy, bulky, very easily damaged and absolutely worthless in our typical environment. It magnified the nighttime light levels so that objects could be seen through the fat telescope's eyepiece. So on a moonlit night the images were clearly seen on a bunker line, but under a heavy canopy with no moonlight coming through, objects could barely be seen or not seen at all. In the heavy jungles, bamboo forests and rubber farms that we worked in, it was useless every night because the moon and starlight could not penetrate the overhead foliage.

To us it was yet another instance of grunts carrying excess weight that provided no advantage. The scope was carried in a fat metal foam-filled briefcase to protect it from moisture and heavy shocks that would render it worthless—wait a minute, it already was worthless. This briefcase was then put into a sandbag with a long cord that acted like a sling so that some poor slob could throw about 12 pounds over his shoulder and hump that bulky thing. If the officers ever had to carry it for three weeks and then use it for only one or two frustrating minutes per mission, it would never have been in the field.

CHAPTER 36

REVENGE

Another time we came back to Quan Loi, got cleaned up, resupplied and slept on cots like usual. We got up early, had an early hot breakfast, climbed into the trucks and were driven to the airstrip just like usual. We were sitting on the ground waiting to hear the slicks fly in. Instead three Shithooks (Chinook helicopters) flew in for us. Now this was a good news/bad news development. Good news – we weren't flying into a hot LZ because they never exposed the large expensive Shithooks to enemy fire. Bad news – we would have a long flight out of our AO, and our mission was to be something different. Naturally, we were all thinking it could easily be something stupid, dangerous and/ or exhausting.

I can't remember anything else, until we found ourselves less than 5 kilometers from the outskirts of Saigon, reinforcing a Ruff Puff (GI-speak for the Vietnamese National Police) highway roadblock. They were inspecting all incoming and outgoing traffic for weapons and supplies. We were their backup, in case one of their inspections turned into a bad and hot situation. All military traffic just flew through the roadblock like we weren't there.

It was actually great duty; we were just stretched out on the side embankment of the raised road buying Cokes, fresh fruit and other food from the civilians. We were very seldom around civilians. I think this is where I traded a pack of Salem cigarettes for four silk paintings that I later sent home.

We had set up several three-man positions so that there was firepower on both sides of the road and to the front and back of the roadblock. It was a lazy day with no excitement of any kind until a brand new Land Rover was stopped. It was straight from the docks, and it was a beauty. It got the attention of every single soldier.

The driver got out and was speaking French to the Ruff Puffs. Suddenly everything changed. We all instantly hated the driver and the Rover. Our AO was in rubber plantation territory. When Vietnam was a French colony, our area of Vietnam was developed into vast rubber plantations, and these plantations were now owned and operated by French Nationals. All of us GIs hated the French because they were paying the NVA with hard currency for protection from interruptions to their rubber production. This currency would be used to purchase arms and other war materials that would then be then be used against us. Of course this did not stop the NVA from traveling through the rubber plantations to move their men and materials. So we would hunt them in the rubber, and every time we would damage a rubber tree in a firefight, the US government would be forced to pay the French owners $600 per damaged tree. The French paid the NVA for protection, and that money was used against the grunts; the French did not restrict the NVA movements in their rubber farms but then charged our government $600 per tree for any damage that occurred in a firefight. This French payment scheme was a very personal affront to the soldiers of the 1st Division, and we hated everything French in Vietnam because of it.

About a minute after the arrival of the French Rover, we heard the whine and rumble of three M113 APCs (Armored Personnel Carriers), coming from Saigon and approaching the roadblock wide open. These US APCs were also straight from the docks, brand new with unblemished paint and no unit markings on them. They were heading north as replacements for some lucky mechanized unit. Zoooooooooooooooom!! and the first one was gone. One hundred yards later, zoooooooooooooooooooooooooom!! and the second one just flew by. Three seconds later ZoooooooooooBANG!!ooooooooom!! and the third one was long gone. Wow! Was that fun to watch! The only slight imperfection of that inspiring sight was that the third APC had hit the back of that beautiful Land Rover about four inches in from the edge. The car jumped forward about four to six feet and was now slowly moving forward towards my position. The entire left side of the car had been moved forward about six inches, the left side glass was shattered, but from every side except the left side, the car was still a beauty.

The Frenchman flew into a rage. He started to scream at the Ruff Puffs but soon realized that there was not the slightest possibility that these little Puffs could do anything. His thoughts next turned to us; after all we were American soldiers, and our fellow soldiers had done the dastardly deed.

But we were nowhere near finished with our laughter and our cheering. He stood there for a second or two, and then he just seemed to explode, flailing his arms and kicking his feet in the air. He turned and with straight legs, long strides and pumping arms, he started heading for an American position.

He got one to two steps forward when he heard about 12 to 14 weapons simultaneously becoming locked and loaded. He froze, paused for an instant—then his shoulders sagged and he slowly walked back over to the Ruff Puffs. There would be no help from the Americans today.

CHAPTER 37

OUR CO'S STUPIDITY CAUSES MIKE PLATOON CASUALTIES

In both the Lai Khe and the Quan Loi AOs, we had a number of operations in bamboo forests. Working in bamboo was a mixed bag depending upon the season and the type of bamboo. During the wet season, all of the plants were lush, and it was stifling-humid and so dense it was very tough to walk through. In the dry season, many varieties (perhaps all?) shed their leaves, and the sun would shine through on us baking us like we were in an oven. The bare plants made walking a bit easier, but the sun was much more direct and hotter and the bamboo still did not allow a breeze to find us. Since the leaves had fallen off we had to walk through about 12 to 16 inches of dry leaves.

I remember two distinct varieties of bamboo. First there was what I will call "clump bamboo." A clump forms where the plants grow in thick bunches from 2 to 6 feet in diameter with usually some space between the clumps. The space would vary with the maturity of the forest and perhaps with the different types of clump bamboo. The second kind had the plants spaced like grass plants—that is, evenly spaced and very close together. This type was often very difficult to walk in, and we often needed the point squad to use their machetes to cut a path for the platoon. The forests could be many square miles with

Bamboo forest (Courtesy pixabay.com.)

occasional clearings that would vary in size. Wherever these clearings would occur, the bamboo plants would seek the sunlight and grow out and down to the ground, forming an almost impregnable wall into the clearing.

On May 9th 1969, we were saddled up and waiting for some choppers on the Quan Loi airstrip, getting ready for a routine operation. We had been there since before daylight, but the choppers hadn't arrived, nor had they contacted us for a couple of hours. Our CO was the most worthless one we ever had, and he was fuming. Several hours later the choppers finally showed up, and we took off and landed in our LZ uneventfully. The whole company was on the ground within an hour, but the old man (CO) was still hopping mad. He was obsessed with making up those lost hours we had spent on the tarmac.

We were preparing to form up to leave the LZ when he ordered us into a single file formation. He insisted we would make better time through the bamboo if we moved in single file rather than using the double column. That was true because with a double file the columns are going to travel only as fast as the slowest column, since the two points had to be kept even with each other. Unfortunately, in a single file you are giving up all of the advantages of the two-column formation: balanced fire power, fast reaction time to an enemy attack and a quicker response of fire power and leadership to the enemy attack. Forget that; he was determined to make up that lost time.

So off we went into the bamboo forest in single file with Mike platoon in the lead and the old man yelling in his radio at our point men to move faster. We trekked for an hour or so, and our company was stretched way out (each man was about 10-15 feet behind the man in front of him); as a result, we were all getting spooked. We were breaking all sorts of best practices now. We were all hoping that our luck would hold out that day and that the following day the CO would be over his dumbass problem.

I was walking approximately nine or ten guys behind the point man when our luck ran out. Our point made contact up front and to the right. I heard a number of AKs (enemy AK-47 assault rifles), a few US M16 rifles and some other various guns. Damn!

Now we were going to pay the price for moving in single file. Everybody was running forward through the bamboo towards the contact, but it was taking valuable time. If we had been in two columns, we could have almost doubled our initial fire power in just a few seconds because the men on the left column would have just run a few meters across the formation left to right from their column to the point of attack. Now men had to run 20 to 50 or 60 yards in heavy bamboo to get to a position so they could lay down some helpful fire. The men of the initial contact were on their own for a much longer time period than normal, and they were taking heavier casualties because of it.

All of the men behind me were running past me because they had an easier time running and crashing through the bamboo with their rifles compared to my bulky machine gun. I caught up with Mike Humlicek, who was also struggling in the bamboo, because his radio pack and antenna were catching on the thick bamboo. Finally Mike and I caught up to men that had run past us as they were laying down fire across a small clearing to the area from where some small arms fire was coming. It was then decided that a base of fire at the enemy be laid down by part of Lima platoon on our right. Simultaneously the men from Mike platoon would gather in the clearing and form an assault line and move towards the enemy small arms fire (this is a classic small unit infantry tactic).

So all of us from Mike platoon started to tunnel, wrestle and fight our way through the very dense bamboo foliage growing down at the edge of the clearing in order to begin moving across the clearing. Most of them eventually got through OK, but Mike and I were on our hands and knees trying to get through a very small hole in the bush just above the ground. Mike had his antenna caught on some bamboo branches, and I was reaching forward and over him to untangle his antenna. Jimmy White, my assistant gunner, was behind me ready to do the same for me. Lima was continuing to lay down a base of fire into the point of initial contact.

Just then all hell broke loose, and I mean full-blown hell! Directly across from us and to our left-front, a bit down from the point of first contact, more enemy fire just exploded. Before, there had been some AKs; now there were additional AKs, and they were joined by two or three machine guns. Holy shit! We rarely ran into machine guns, and now there were two or three – what was going on? Right away many of those who got through the thick bamboo faster than Mike and I did were hit; this included several men from our point squad, our lieutenant, our sniper and others. Mike tried to move, but he still had his radio antenna stuck. Next the ground around the three of us erupted with bullets and debris. The enemy had just spotted a radio and machine gun right next to each other, and they saw that we were stuck. They were frantically throwing everything they could at these high priority targets. We were caught and couldn't go forward, so we tried to crawl backward. All I could think was "Please don't get hung up; please don't get hung up," meaning that I didn't want my gun or Mike's radio to get caught on the bamboo going backwards.

So much fire was coming at us that we couldn't see or hear anything. The enemy fire just kept increasing in intensity; there were more and more enemy soldiers firing at us by the second. The rest of our company was catching up and running towards the fire fight and adding more fire. The sound was incredible, along with the dust, smell and confusion.

Meanwhile, Mike, Jimmy and I pulled back out of the hole in the brush about five to ten feet into a very, very slight dip in the ground. The bullets were beyond belief above us but not hitting us. I cannot explain how we survived the 30 to 45 seconds it took for us to get unhooked from the bamboo and back to the small dip. The enemy knew where we were and continued to fire amazing amounts of small arms fire at us, but the bullets were just slightly above our bodies. I could literally feel the air from the rounds as they just missed me. We all had no choice but to just hunker down and snuggle into the earth while the fire fight continued to rage on.

I think we were stuck there for 30 minutes, but it could have been 10 or 50—I simply don't know. Meanwhile some air support arrived, and soon we had two Cobra gunships working on the far side of the clearing. That slowed down the enemy fire on us a bit and allowed the three of us to move behind a termite hill, which is like a four-foot pile of concrete, and collect our wits. As we were stuck out there, the other two platoons had organized in our area and relieved what was left of Mike platoon from most of the fighting. This allowed Mike platoon to get organized behind them.

Now we had a roaring stalemate. Two forces were fiercely fighting each other across a clearing. We had air support, but we also had a several KIAs (killed in action) and wounded in a bomb crater in the middle of the clearing. We had to figure out a way to get them out of there. Mike platoon moved forward and again joined the fight. Part of Lima platoon then went on a sweeping action to the right and a part of November platoon did the same on the left. They moved to the left and right to try to go around the enemy's side or rear to either contain them or get them in a cross fire. Instead, what they found were more enemy positions in line with the first ones.

We finally had the whole picture. We had been practically running in single file through the bamboo as the old man was yelling at the point men to go faster when we inadvertently ended up on a parallel course 30 feet from the bunker line of a large, occupied enemy basecamp. Our point men didn't see the camouflaged bunkers as they were rushing to keep the CO happy. The first enemy contact was a few soldiers with AKs to draw us into an offensive formation. Then with more of us ready to assault them, they opened up on us with their heavier guns in camouflaged bunkers and brought additional enemy soldiers into the fight.

On our side, we were slow to react because the CO had us so strung out with the damned single file formation. It took forever to get our men and fire power in place and, all the while, Mike platoon got chewed up. We now knew that we were outnumbered; without our air support, the company would have been surrounded by a superior force.

This is the point at which I lose my mental timeline. All I remember is that our company tried everything we could to suppress the enemy fire and retrieve the dead and wounded. When the air support arrived, the company started throwing smoke grenades in front of our line so that that the pilots could determine our line formation and then bring in their support in a specified direction and at a given distance from our smoke. They came in low, close and with guns wide open and helped us considerably right away. I recall several times when an avalanche of very hot machine gun shell casings would fall on us and burn the hell out our necks and backs.

One bad result of the air support was that the smoke grenades, which we used to indicate our locations to the gunships, started the 12 or 14 inches of dried bamboo leaves on fire. That in turn started the whole bamboo forest on fire. Our entire company was engaged in a fierce firefight with a very large enemy force, and we were rolling around trying to stay low while sweeping burning leaves and twigs with our legs and arms and choking on the smoke. Our eyes were watering so we couldn't see, and it was hell on earth for a very long hour or two. Finally the firestorm ran out of fuel, slowed down and mostly went out except for the embers.

At one point, one or two LAWs (a one shot, throw-away bazooka) were fired at the enemy bunkers by our CO, but he forgot to check to his rear to make sure no one was behind him where the hot gasses from the bazooka rocket were directed. The LAW had no impact on the firefight, due to either a poor aim or a good bunker, but he managed to burn a man or two behind him with the hot rocket blast.

The company continued to fight hard. A number of fighting tactics at the enemy bunker line, along with the air support, resulted in some easing of enemy fire. However, the one enemy machine gun that had the crater filled with our wounded in its field of fire was still hunkered down and going strong.

At this point Pete Bernardini, Mike Platoon's medic, crawled up beside me, and since medics weren't armed, he asked me for my .45 pistol for a bit of protection. He told me he was going to try to crawl out to the wounded in the crater. So he took my pistol, shoved it in a pocket and crept past me into the hell. Doc soon got shot several times in the arm and shoulder and was stopped. He was in bad shape and was fading out when a couple of Mike Platoon men low-crawled out, grabbed his feet and drug him back behind cover. There he was treated by another medic and kept from bleeding out. He was medivaced out later.

Finally it was agreed that the only way to stop the fire from that bunker was to have me, and then Jimmy White, return to that small depression where we and Mike Humlicek had been pinned down for so long. I was to shoot my gun right down the throat of the bunker. It certainly had been made clear with all of our prior attacks on it that afternoon that firing at any angle other than straight-in would not silence that enemy machine gun. There would be no recovering our dead and wounded without stopping that gun. So the old man came over to me and told me to silence that machine gun.

First, Jimmy and I made an extra-long starter belt. Usually I carried a belt with 100 to 125 rounds, but for this job we snapped on another 100 rounds. I told Jimmy that I was going to jump over to the dip and that if I was able to fire the first 100 rounds that he should then join me. The difference this time was that we were not going to be eating dirt and staying low, but we were going to be much higher profiles in order to aim and fire our machine gun. It was going to be a shootout, but the enemy had cover and we didn't. On the other hand, I was going to surprise him because no one had been directly in front of him firing at him all afternoon.

I dove into the depression and started firing straight out front and very low just in front of the far edge of the clearing. Firing high accomplishes nothing; when firing low, one is more likely to hit the target, cause casualties with ricochets and at least throw debris to cause confusion and interfere with the machine gunner's sight. I received no return fire so I just kept my fire concentrated on the black hole I had been targeting. Jimmy joined me, and we just kept continuously firing at a sustained rate. A sustained rate means that I would fire a 5 to 8-round burst with a one to two second pause between the bursts. This saves ammunition yet doesn't allow the enemy time to get back into position to return fire.

Since the last enemy machine gun seemed to be silenced for the moment, volunteers from Mike platoon ran across the clearing and dove under my fire and into the crater. When the wounded were dragged and carried back behind our line, our medics could finally start treating their injuries and prepping them for evacuation. The only soldier that we didn't retrieve was a KIA that was way out front next to an enemy bunker.

This activity took some time, and our platoon just kept collecting ammo from the other machine guns in the company and throwing it to Jimmy. By the time the last of the wounded had been retrieved, Jimmy had a pile of brass the size of a bushel basket. At that point, I was pulling the trigger with alternating fingers because the gun had become so hot from the extended period of firing.

It was now late and darkness was about to be on us, so the company was ordered to back away from the enemy basecamp. We pulled away from the camp several hundred meters and started to dig in, setting up a night defensive position (NDP). We knew there were plenty of enemy soldiers close by; we also knew they would keep attacking us. As we were digging in, the medics were patching and stabilizing our wounded because medevac choppers had been called for the evacuation.

This night was the first time I ever watched a man die. I had seen a lot of death and a lot of dying from a distance, but I had never seen a man die when I was with him. I was squatted down beside my Platoon Leader as he was trying to give some directions to his squad leaders; I observed that he was going downhill fast.

Three or four hours earlier, he had been hit several times when Mike Platoon had tried to make a frontal assault. He had

Lt. Pratt

been pinned in the bomb crater for several hours before he got any aid from a medic. Then his Mike Platoon friends had pulled him out of the crater under my covering fire. Still later he was carried with the rest of our wounded as we retreated. He was now with the other wounded in the center of the company waiting for a medevac as the company was digging in for a long night.

I got word that he had sent for his squad leaders so I left Jimmy and the ammo bearer as they continued to dig in. The other squad leaders and I found him, and he was very quiet and mostly confused. We silently gathered around him and listened to him trying to direct us, but instead we just watched him fail. He had held on through all of those hours and moves, and now he was dying. He was in mid-sentence when his essence simply left his body through his eyes, and he was gone. We called the medic, and he came over and said he was dead. We all got up and went back to our jobs. I remembered I felt sincere sorrow for his family, but I just went back to work. I was six months in-country by then, and I knew I had to leave this death behind and go back to work to keep from getting overrun that night.

It was totally dark now, and since there was no clearing where we were located, the Medevac helicopters had to hover above us and use a jungle penetrator to evacuate our injured. A penetrator is an egg-shaped metal cage into which a wounded person would be inserted in a sitting position; then he would be winched up and into the chopper. This was a slow and very dangerous operation because of the enemy numbers and location all around us. A loaded chopper needs to have forward speed to gain rapid elevation and there was no direction for our choppers to get forward speed without flying over enemy ground troops. We did have a gunship working our perimeter during this time and much of the night to slow down the enemy attacks against us.

After the choppers had taken our wounded, we received some emergency resupply flights. We had been through a long hot day. It had been a dry and hot day, and water was consumed at a higher rate. Most men carried five quarts. We were all very disciplined in our water use, but today we had used more than usual. We had been going fast in file, and then we experienced one of the longest and fiercest firefights many of us had ever been in; we had fought in a forest fire, and many men like me had had one of his two quart water bladders get punctured and had lost all of the water in them. Our ammo supply was also critical. So choppers came in and hovered over the central area of the NDP and kicked out water, canteens, ammo and a few other miscellaneous supplies.

One large crate of ammo landed on a Mike Platoon soldier and broke his shoulder and caused internal injuries, so we had to call in another medevac mission. One of the miscellaneous items in our resupply flights was a new machine gun barrel for me since I had completely "carbonned" up my barrel when I fired all of those rounds at the bunker. I started to clean my gun when we were digging in and discovered that when my gun cooled down it no longer fired! I had so much carbon in the area that makes the gun continue to fire automatically that it was frozen. The part that shuttles back and forth directing the gases backward to force the bolt back, reject the spent round, load a new round and cock the gun was frozen in place. So I ordered a new barrel that was changed in 15 seconds, but until that supply flight got to us, the company was without my machine gun.

Meanwhile, tactical air support was called in and for much of the first part of the night either the Navy or Air Force was chewing up the area of the basecamp. We had our skirmishes all night, but the close air support kept them from massing and over-running us. That was our first night of no sleep.

The next morning we got up and went back to their basecamp to recover the KIA that we left behind. Petey, David Peterson, was our sniper. As I walked back into that scene, I found it incredibly shocking. The first time I had walked into the area, less than 24 hours before, it was just a typical bamboo forest with a small clearing—a characteristic setting seen by all of us hundreds of times. After eight to ten hours of fierce small arms combat, close air support and tactical air strikes the little area was transformed into a completely charred, bleak, moonscape. And there lay Petey.

He was on the far side of the clearing right up against a bunker port (hole that is used to shoot through) that he had obviously not seen. He lay on his stomach with one of his knees bent so that his lower leg and foot were perfectly vertical. Up to half of his uniform was burned off and some of his skin was charred. In addition, since he was right up against the port, he had about a third of his torso shot away by the enemy machine gunner inside the bunker. He had ended up functioning like some sandbags protecting the front of the bunker and the enemy within.

Petey's death was the hardest death for me that year, and much of Mike Platoon felt the same. He was a sweet, nice, naive, clean-cut, 18 year-old draftee from Minnesota. Every single person in Mike Platoon liked him; no one teased him or made fun of his naiveté. He liked and respected everyone in the platoon, and those feelings were reciprocated by all of us in return. Less than a month earlier he had returned from Hawaii after seeing his parents for his R and R week. The Hawaii slots were almost exclusively reserved for married soldiers, but our clerk had secured Petey a trip to see his parents. He had never fired a gun of any sort before he came into the army, yet he was the best shot in the company. He had crawled out into that hell to try to save someone and lost his life.

Mike platoon filed over to his body, and some of his friends put him on a poncho liner and started to carry him back home. We carried him for much of the day and kept him safe through several ambushes until we got to a small clearing to send him away. We all thought, “Go in peace, Petey.”

Thankfully, for some reason no bombs from the tactical air strike had landed in Petey’s little area, but there was a great deal of damage to the rest of the enemy basecamp. Usually we would sweep the camp and look for some intel, but we knew we were going to have our hands full that day. There were still many NVA around us, and they wanted our hides. They had all abandoned the basecamp way before the air strikes and were hiding in the area, with plans to engage us as often as possible.

For the next two days and nights, that was exactly what took place. We zigzagged through the jungles and forests, and they tried to anticipate where we would be and then ambush us. We had many small firefights and a couple a bit larger, depending on the size of their ambush, but our point men did a great job of keeping us out of real trouble. Every night we made an NDP and set up predetermined defensive artillery points all around our position so that we could have instant artillery support during the night if and when we needed it.

CHAPTER 38

THE DISASTER CONTINUES

Finally on the fourth day, we pretty much left them behind, and we had very little or no contact that day. Late in the afternoon, we got picked up and flown back to Quan Loi. Man, were we exhausted! We were trucked back to our company area and stumbled into our tents, sat on our cots and started cleaning and inventorying our gear. We were all a mess but especially Mike Platoon. We had ruined or lost a lot of gear that first day, and it took some time to clean up and compile a list of our needs for Supply.

Next we showered and had a hot meal, ahhhhhhh! Then we were given our requested gear from Supply. We were once again field-ready. Bedtime! Oh, did that cot feel good. We all went to sleep very early; my guess was 8:30 or 9:00 p.m. Sometime later we heard a few shots on the bunker line but thought little of it; hearing a few shots from the bunker line was not unusual.

All of a sudden, at around 11:00, there was severe yelling: "GET UP AND SADDLE UP!" Over and over someone was going to every tent and yelling. Oh fuck! We were prepared to go in a minute or two while our platoon leaders were talking with the CO. The platoon leaders returned to their platoons and informed us that an enemy force had quietly penetrated the wire and was pouring into our basecamp. A large section of our bunker line was in their control, and there were enemy troops in two areas inside the camp. Load up!

We were the only infantry in the whole damned basecamp, and we had to go fight the enemy again. We were trucked about a half a mile, where we dismounted. Lima and November platoons were directed into two separate objectives, a large open grassy area and a Battalion motor pool. A motor pool is a large parking lot filled with large army trucks, smaller trucks, jeeps and trailers. These were the two areas in which the NVA had reorganized inside the wire, and we had to push them back to the wire.

The plan was for Lima to clear out the motor pool area, November to clear out the field and, since Mike was at low strength from our casualties from several days earlier, we would be the ready reserve for both platoons. November platoon entered the grassy area and found the NVA scattered throughout the field. They quickly realized that if they had a profile above the grass they would get fired on by the enemy. So they formed four or five columns and started to fan out through the field. Each column low-crawled about eight to ten yards, at which time the point man would throw a fragmentation grenade in front of him about eight to ten yards. He would then crawl through the new clean, enemy-free space to about five yards past the grenade blast and then do the same process again. The men behind just kept passing up the frags and following behind. In about an hour November had control of the grassy area, and the enemy had retreated back to the bunker line. November platoon suffered no or few minor casualties from that action.

Lima meanwhile had divided into a number of fire teams and was working its way through the motor pool. Each team would make contact with an enemy soldier or group and use a fire and maneuver tactic which had half the team firing on the enemy while the other half would move forward. Then they would lay down the fire until the other half would advance ahead of them. Eventually one part of the team would get past the truck or jeep and shoot the enemy. This effectively drove the remaining enemy out of the area and back to the bunker line.

Our company then formed into a blocking force, effectively sealing the enemy from being able to enter into the basecamp. In addition, Spooky had been called in. Spooky was an AC-47, a very serious military version of the DC-3, with three mini-guns mounted in the cargo area that shot out through windows in the left side of the plane. Each of these guns could shoot 100 rounds per SECOND. Spooky would also drop illumination flares to light up the battle area so the enemy could be seen.

These planes would orbit around a battlefield where they fired 3 to 5 second bursts into their target area; each burst would saturate the area with 900 to 1500 rounds. This plane was definitely keeping the NVA from leaving Quan Loi and definitely keeping any additional troops from coming into the base. Our exhausted company had the attackers trapped in 10 or 12 of Quan Loi's bunkers by 2:00 a.m., with very light losses. The enemy was going nowhere, and the basecamp was safe from this bunker line breach.

The Quan Loi basecamp was our brigade's headquarters (1st brigade, 1st Infantry Division). Our brigade's CO was usually a Brigadier (one star) General or a full colonel. He was in command of five combat infantry battalions (20 on-line companies), one of which was an armored infantry unit. He also had command of an armored Cavalry REGIMENT, an engineering BATTALION that had Rome Plows, and he had full access to any kind of air power he wanted that could destroy those bunkers and the enemy troops. Under his direct command he could have called in the armored Cavalry with their M60 tanks to annihilate the bunkers and NVA soldiers, or he could have had the Rome plows just push down the bunkers and NVA soldiers with great safety or he could have used bombs or napalm and destroyed them in a safe manner for us. He could have made any or all of these things happen. Instead . . .

At 2:30 a.m. over the battalion radio we received orders on the battalion frequency to take back the bunker line.

Once again Lima and November Platoons split up and started fighting bunker to bunker from each end to take the bunkers back from the NVA. Mike platoon was split again, following the two other platoons, but most of Mike was pretty much out of the heavy fighting. By 4:30 a.m., all of the bunkers were in our control; the enemy troops were either out of the wire and dead from Spooky or dead inside the wire. We then set up fighting positions on top of the bunkers for the rest of the night. We were on top of the bunkers because, from that position, we could

My gun on a bunker at Quan Loi

see over the lip of the valley edge and farther down the slope. Probably the reason the enemy attack had taken place at that location on the bunker line was that the attackers could get closer to the bunker line without being seen by the men inside the bunkers. Most of the other bunkers on the base had much better visibility than those we had just retaken.

For the next hour or so we just watched Spooky drop illumination flares and occasionally fire into the valley in front of us. At some point near daybreak, Spooky flew off station and said good bye to Quan Loi. A few minutes later, we had a rocket attack along the bunker line, and we all dove into the bunkers. We were crawling out a few minutes later when someone from our company told us to rally (gather) at an abandoned building a few yards past the end of the bunkers we had taken back.

So we picked up our gear and dragged our sorry asses down to the rally point. I remember so clearly lounging on the ground watching the straggling, scruffy, pathetic-looking guys singly or in twos and threes walking up the road towards us. Company A had just won yet another face-to-face fight with the enemy that surely gave pride to our leaders, but I saw no pride or celebration in these men. Instead I just watched filthy and exhausted men slowly gather at the rally point. No victory was felt here.

It took a few minutes to make a small group. Soon the arrival of men at the rally point slowed up and then it just stopped. I started to think, "What's keeping the rest of them – I want to go back and get some sleep."

Max Hanson, the only other surviving M60 gunner

And then it hit me – this was everybody! Our group had been decimated fighting an enemy entrenched in our bunkers. Soon all of us understood. We didn't know our casualty rate last night because we ended up in small groups on the bunkers, but now it hit us. We started to talk among the platoons, and we soon discovered that the two remaining company medics had been killed, four of the six machine gun crews were killed, and on and on. Four days ago, we had been at normal strength of 95 to105 men in the field; at this rally point we had 28 left. Ironically, Mike Platoon had the highest strength now. A Company had won the battle, but the pathetic men who had done the fighting had been betrayed by their own promotion-hungry leadership and were wasted.

Our Brigade Commander had had his basecamp safe in this area by 2:00 a.m. with light casualties. At that time, there was no way the enemy could mount any kind of threat through this huge hole in the wire with us as a blocking force between the enemy and the base. Moreover, Spooky was at that time on station over Quan Loi to ensure no NVA reinforcements could be brought in anywhere. As I have discussed before, the Brigade CO had many options to get rid of the enemy safely the next morning. I will never believe any other explanation for his decision to have us take back our own bunkers other than he did not want to have a paragraph in his morning report that a small part of his bunker line was not in his control. That pocket of enemy soldiers was not a threat to his command, but they could have become a threat to his career. That little notation might be noticed on his next promotion review.

He was more worried about not having 12 bunkers under his control, even with the basecamp being safe; than he was about having an infantry company experience 60% casualties and being declared as Not Combat Ready. There were NO consequences for casualties in the 1969 draft INFANTRY.

They weren't done with us yet. During the early morning, before the company was ordered to rally, the company CO and the battalion CO were discussing our casualties over the radio. The battalion CO told our CO to keep the men from licking their wounds and make them take a long walk to get their minds off the fight. A few minutes later when our CO finally joined us at the rally point and saw that there were only 28 of us left, his RTO heard him say softly to himself, "Oh my God." He obviously hadn't realized the extent of our casualties earlier when he was speaking with battalion.

In my opinion, our captain should have told his boss that his men had not slept in four nights and needed rest more than a morning walk to get their minds off of the night battle. But instead, he ordered the company to saddle up and patrol around the entire basecamp. So we walked to the nearest gate and started our patrol around the basecamp. Quan Loi was built on a ridge so the terrain for us walking around it was all sloped so we walked the entire multiple mile patrol on a bare, hot side hill. The whole area had been bulldozed bare which meant we were out in the full sun (not something we were used to) and on very rocky terrain. We were also edgy about some nervous rear-guard greenie on the bunker line taking a shot at us because we were in front of him. It was a long, hot and exhausting walk. We went all the way around the basecamp and did not find one single enemy body; they had carried and dragged all of their dead back into the bush. We heard later when other companies did operations close in and around Quan Loi that there were many fresh graves in the jungle across the valley from where we had fought.

Upon returning from our patrol, we received more devastating news. There had been another but smaller breach in the wire. A group of NVA soldiers and sappers had sneaked through the wire on the far side of basecamp, where they were probably planning to attack the large field artillery units located in that area. A sapper is a soldier that carries a satchel full of explosives that is used to destroy large targets. He is a human-delivered bomb. Unfortunately, they had come across our company's Mortar Platoon and killed or wounded all but one man. Except for Jim Bevard, who returned from his R and R, not one of the wounded men ever returned to mortars. This was a real kick in the gut because we all considered the Mortar Platoon as a much safer assignment.

The men assigned to mortars seldom humped in the boonies and were inside the wire most of the time. It was an unspoken understanding that those of us who took those high risk (high casualty) jobs like pulling point, carrying radios (RTO) or manning machine guns would eventually get pulled off the rifle platoons and have the CO assign us to a much more secure job than we presently had. Assignment to the Mortars was one of the best because the CO would make the assignment himself within the company, and we would not have to wait for an opening in one of the Battalion rear jobs. Those jobs could be filled with a soldier from our company or one of the other companies in our battalion. When we heard about the mortar platoon's casualties, we all felt like someone had just cut our safety net.

Now, including our losses from the Mortars, we had lost more than 70% of our strength in four days. We had gone from about 110 or 120 combat troops, including those in mortars, to 28, plus a few walking wounded. Alpha Company First of the Second Infantry was no longer classified as Combat Ready.

CHAPTER 39

MEDALS AND DECORATIONS

Many civilians might think that, following the events just described, all sorts of medals and honors would have been awarded to "Our American Heroes." This notion may be true and it may not be true. The funny thing about medals and awards is that sometimes they represent great bravery and super-charged events, sometimes they represent a job of administration especially well done in the states (not unlike a year-end bonus in business) and sometimes they are a fraud. To sort this out a bit, let's consider my small handful of awards from my military experiences.

First, in Basic, I qualified as expert with an M14 rifle. This rather surprised me since I had fired a rifle very few times before Basic. Next in AIT (Advanced Infantry Training) I qualified as expert again, this time on the M16, yet another surprise. Maybe their training techniques were better than we all gave them credit for. The third weapon on which we ALL had to qualify was the M60 machine gun. My training company spent an entire day on the machine gun range getting ready to qualify a few days later. The day arrived to qualify, and I was put on KP (kitchen slave duty) so I never qualified on the M60.

As Graduation Day approached, we were all handed some stuff to put on our Dress Uniforms for the big Graduation Parade. My stuff was a National Defense ribbon and an Expert Weapons Badge with an M14, an M16 and an M60 bar attached to the badge. There was no special ceremony, there were no congratulations, there were no orders—just "here you go and put those things on your uniform here and here." The irony of that event was that later when I was on-line in Vietnam I was assigned as an M60 machine gunner, the only weapon for which, in actuality, I was never "qualified."

The next event concerning my awards was about eight or nine months later when I was in Vietnam and had been on-line for seven months. Our Platoon Leader came into our platoon tent late one afternoon as we were cleaning our weapons. We had just gotten back to basecamp, and we were doing our late afternoon/early morning turnabout. He had a paper in his hand and he read off a list of names of men in Mike platoon and he said, "Well you've now got your CIBs" (Combat Infantry Badges). A CIB was awarded to an infantryman after 30 days of combat when assigned to an infantry battalion in a combat theater. This CIB name-reading event happened every so often, but we never saw the orders or the awards.

A couple of months later, a few weeks after those four horrific days of heavy casualties, there were rumors that there were a few people up for some awards. To my knowledge no one knew who the men were or what the awards were. Many months later, the news just materialized that the men that had crawled under my machine gun rounds and pulled the wounded from the crater, as well as Jimmy and I, were awarded the Bronze Star with V device (V meaning for a valorous action). There were other medals given to the survivors of Lima and November Platoons too for their hard fought time clearing out the enemy from the bunkers at Quan Loi basecamp. The only survivor from Mortar Platoon was awarded a Silver Star for his hand-to-hand fight with the enemy at the mortar area and for somehow surviving that night. There was no ceremony; there were no congratulations, no orders, no medals—nothing for us. Additionally, there were probably a number of posthumous medals awarded to many of the dead and wounded that never returned to A Company, but we were never told any of that information.

My final awards event was in the states at the very end of my career. I was given a new Class A uniform with all of my awards on it. It was in Oakland that I learned that I had been awarded a second Bronze Star and an Air Medal. Another surprise was that my nonexistent M-60 machine gun qualification was now demoted a step to a sharpshooter badge from an expert, and that someone had actually created orders for it. Both badges were phony, since I had never actually qualified for either (recall that I had KP duty the day we were to qualify!) There was no ceremony; there were no congratulations—just stuff for our uniforms.

My experience concerning military awards begs this question: What is the function of military awards? I have heard some answers to this question: to bolster the morale of the troops, to encourage high support for the war on the home front and to improve one's army career by increasing his or her promotion points.

In the draft infantry the first function, the notion of bolstering the morale of the troops, was laughable. When in Vietnam, we knew nothing or next to nothing about any of our awards, and most of our leadership didn't appear to give a shit about us or our awards. As to the second function, our awards possibly could have played an important role in maintaining the home front's support for the war. All of the drafted infantry cynics that I hung around with always thought that if the hometown newspaper had seven or eight award pieces for every KIA piece in the hometown press, then the support for the war might be maintained. After all, what town doesn't like heroes? However, as far as I knew, there was not a single article in my hometown paper about me while I was in the military. Maybe it would have been different had I been killed.

But in most of the grunt's opinions, it was the third function that drove the bus. The night that Lima and November platoons were shredded, we heard that the only Silver Star (the third highest medal, which is awarded for "gallantry in action against an enemy") that was awarded to the three rifle platoons was to our lifer First Sergeant. That night he was nowhere near the fighting. The only thing we were aware that he did that night was yell and get us awake, up and ready to fight the enemy. Later, as things got worse, he took the wounded men held back from Mike and made them join the fight. In our company the only DRAFTEE that got a Silver Star was Halpin, the one survivor from Mortars, who fought hand-to-hand with the enemy as the rest of his platoon was killed or seriously wounded. As we were told, another notable Silver Star recipient was the Brigade Commander. He was the commander who, even though he had other low casualty options at his disposal, gave Alpha Company the 2:00 AM order to retake the bunkers, an order that resulted in casualties so high that we were forced to be taken off-line. These three Silver Stars are the only ones that I ever heard about during my one-year tour. I would love to read the descriptions of the valorous deeds performed by these two lifers that compelled someone to substantiate these high awards for gallantry against the enemy. IF NOT ONE of the men that fought and took back those bunkers, 50% of whom ended up as casualties, could meet the criteria for a Silver Star that night, then it is hard for me to believe that the two lifers who were awarded one did anything more valorous.

Each of the lifers was presented his award in formal farewell ceremonies witnessed by at least 100 men as the lifers left for home. In contrast, Halpin was eventually told about his award and never received any public recognition. These awards were lifer candy handed out to lifers by lifers to earn them promotion points and lifer prestige. Remember, everything that had to do with being nominated for or receiving an award was controlled by the lifers. There is a possibility that some of our men did get medals for that difficult night's work, but our company never had any kind of ceremony for them—so much for the morale booster argument for awarding medals.

In no way do I intend to say that an infantry lifer never properly earned a prestigious award or that not a single infantry lifer cared anything for his troops. However, I do wish to go on record as saying that, from my observation, there certainly seemed to be a huge disparity between the actions required for a draftee to earn valorous recognition and the actions required for an infantry lifer to earn recognition.

For thirty five years I thought little about my awards. I think I must have felt that as each piece of lifer candy was given to an undeserving lifer I should subtract a piece of honor or respect for each award I was given. It was the natural outcome of the cynicism that had developed in all of us as we lived in the dual caste system of the 1968-69 draft infantry.

At some point later in my life, I decided that I was pleased that I had a CIB (Combat Infantry Badge). After going through all that shit, the few times I did talk to fellow vets I was glad that I could say I had a CIB. I eventually concluded that the Bronze Stars were for actions that required us to do our best to get our friends and ourselves out of a jam in order to get us all home. But, to me, the Air Medal has come to mean the most, because I believe it signifies the acts that took the most personal courage. It was awarded in recognition of my participation in all of those dangerous aerial insertions. I have come to understand that keeping my cool and focusing on what had to be done, while waiting on the tarmac for the choppers, took *real* courage.

In the process of writing this piece I have finally allowed myself to accept some honor for the awards that I earned. I now understand that the dual set of standards required for a draftee and a lifer didn't diminish my accomplishments. I now view these awards as indications that I contributed my best efforts in trying to get myself and my fellow infantrymen home.

PART 6

REBUILDING ALPHA COMPANY

CHAPTER 40

REASSIGNMENT TO MORTARS

After its huge losses, Alpha Company had to stand down to reorganize and to start receiving huge numbers of replacements. The typical replacement rate would be four to five replacements a week for the entire company. If we had some casualties, we would hope for up to eight or ten. In reality, we needed seventy to eighty men! So we were sent to a camp somewhere else. They let us sleep and play cards for three days while they were determining how many of our wounded would return, how many replacements were needed and how the hell they were going to reorganize and train us into a fighting unit. When a company is comprised of 40 to 50% newbies (and we were going to have more than that) it is not an effective fighting force.

During this three-day stand down, I got into a continuous cribbage game with three other guys. We would play cribbage and then sleep, then play cribbage and then sleep and so on. We did this for three days and nights. We were playing for a dollar a point, two dollars a point if you were skunked and four dollars a point if you were double skunked. For three days, we kept a running score. The lead would change and the point spread would tighten or spread, but we just kept playing. At the end of the stand down, we settled up; I was the big winner and I got less than a dollar. We could not believe it! The winner got less than a buck after three full days of playing. Oh well, no extra money for R and R.

During this down time, the company CO sent word that he wanted to see me. I walked over to his hut and reported to him. He asked me if I was ready to get out of the rifle platoons, and I told him that I was. He asked me to consider being reassigned to our mortar platoon. He told me that I had been a good machine gunner and that I had served the company well. He said that he had a particularly difficult job in rebuilding the mortars because he could not get enough trained mortar men to restore it as an effective platoon. He needed both a person of my rank of Sergeant and someone who could learn a completely new technical skill in a hurry, and he thought that I was his man. He told me to think it over and let him know in an hour. I think that the only reason he gave me a choice was that he knew how much the annihilation of the mortars had spooked the extremely superstitious grunts under his command. I told him I didn't need to think about it and that I was indeed his man.

To us grunts in our battalion, being assigned to mortars was a desirable assignment. Although the 81mm mortar was designed to be carried in the field, the overhead cover that we operated in made it a heavy, useless weapon most of the time. But, it was an effective weapon for basecamp defense and was usually deployed inside basecamps. Although it was not a ticket home, the odds of survival greatly improved for me now that I was going to mortars. This is the day I had been waiting for and the reason I had endured the "painted target on my chest" when I humped the machine gun.

The army has a system for designating the different jobs in the force. I was trained as an 11B which indicated that I was trained as a small arms infantryman. An 11C designation indicates that a person was trained as a mortar crew member. Their training included much of our early training, but the last few weeks they trained as a mortar crewman. There were many more 11Bs trained than 11Cs in 1969. It was common practice in our company and most of the other infantry companies to assign the 11Cs to the rifle platoons and not the mortar platoons. If they proved themselves in the field and took the more dangerous assignments, they were almost always reassigned to the mortars.

Rich Lovejoy, one of my four best friends in Mike Platoon, was a point man and was one of the wounded trapped in the crater that first day of the four-day battle. He had been medically treated and had returned to the company. He had been trained as an 11C, and he too was called in to see the CO. So Rich and I were the first of our group of four buddies to get out of the rifle platoon and into a bit safer place. Mike Humlicek really wanted to get into Mortars with us, and Rich and I tried hard to get him there. However, ultimately, the CO wanted Rich because of his 11C training and wanted me because of my E-5 rank. He also wanted some continuity for himself in the field so he kept Mike as his RTO. Our fourth buddy Jim also continued to be an RTO in the field.

Some time later, during a joint operation with a mechanized infantry unit, both Mike and Jim were riding on an APC when it hit a mine. The explosion blew all of the men off the "track" or APC, some going straight up and some getting blown sideways into the bush. Jim went sideways and was treated for a back injury. Because of those injuries, he received a Purple Heart and a medical profile that made him ineligible for combat duty. So he got a job back in the rear with our battalion, driving the battalion CO—a jewel of a job! Jim told us that he had a back injury before he was drafted and that he tried to use it to prevent him from being drafted, to no avail. Now, because of the blast, the army could "see" an injured back (it may have well been an additional injury), and he was relieved from combat status.

Mike, on the other hand, was blown straight up and landed back on (actually into) the APC and never missed a day on-line. Every person that landed off of the track was given a medical profile and everyone that landed back on the track stayed on-line. A bit later, Mike finally got a rear job in battalion artillery as an RTO. He began operating the same radio in artillery that he had formerly been talking to from the field when ordering artillery support.

The company was returned to Quan Loi and started to receive new replacements. As they came in, there started to be enough new 11Cs (trained in mortars) for them to start training us on the fundamentals of being mortar men. I was a sergeant so I was assigned to be one of the two gunners in mortars. This meant that even though the other two crew members on my gun (or tube) were 11Cs, I was the leader of that gun crew.

Halpin and Bevard, the only men to return to mortars

The mortars platoon was located in a different part of the basecamp than the rest of A Company. It was about a mile away from the company headquarters and our rifle platoon's sleeping area. It was with a very strange mix of emotions that Rich and I left our friends from Mike platoon to go work and live in mortars. The difficulty was that we knew we would not see them very often since we were located a mile or so apart when they were in the camp. When the company finally got up to strength and started going out in the field, it would suddenly be even tougher to see any of those friends. It was especially difficult to leave Mike and Jim because they would still be humping the boonies with their heads stuck out carrying those radios. That was my first dose of survivor's guilt.

I stated earlier that there was only one survivor in mortars the night of the attack on the platoon. This is true; however, we actually had two experienced mortar men to help rebuild the platoon. Jim Bevard from Waterloo, Iowa was another survivor because he had been on R and R in Hawaii to meet his wife and new son. He landed in Quan Loi the day after the attack and was stunned to find his entire platoon but one wiped out and the company decimated.

Most of the new mortar platoon was comprised of 11Cs, and I was the only new 11B. Jim Bevard was the other 11B and had been Mike Platoon's and then the CO's RTO when I first joined the company. Army slang for the 11Bs was *Bravos* and for 11Cs was *Charlies*. Jim and I were the only Bravos in the platoon. Since we had only two experienced mortar men out of a 15-man platoon, we had a lot of training to do. However, with absolutely no mortar training, I had the most to learn.

A mortar platoon was comprised of three squads—two gun squads and a Fire Direction Center (FDC) squad. The FDC was located in a bunker and had several radios that were tuned to several different frequencies. One was tuned to the artillery net where each artillery unit had a call sign. On this net if we heard a call to our call sign we would answer the call and get the information for our fire mission. By the time this net called us, the officers in artillery had already cleared the area (made sure no friendlies were in the area) where the requesting unit wanted to direct the fire mission.

Upon a call for a fire mission, the men in FDC would plot on a map fixed to a fire calculator the location of the area in which the ground unit wanted the mortar rounds to land. Using our FDC calculator, the men in the FDC would then determine the settings used by the gunner to set the optical sight on the tube and the number of powder charges used on each mortar round. With this information, the crew would begin their directed activities to get the gun ready for the fire mission. The gunner would enter the data into the gun's optical sight.

81mm mortar tube, base plate, optical sight and tripod (Courtesy http://publicdomainvectors.org.)

The second crew member would pull the correct type of round (high explosive, illumination, white phosphorous, etc.) out of the storage area and remove all extra powder charges from the round so that the correct number of charges remained on the round. The third member of the crew would grab the bipod legs of the gun and swing

Gun ring and FDC Bunker at Fire Base Pine Ridge

the tube around until the tube was pointing in the direction of the mission. He would then work with the gunner to move the bipod up and down, left and right, until the gunner could see the sighting rods through his sight. Then with the information already dialed into his sight, the gunner would make the final adjustments by manipulating the adjusting knobs on the bipod legs until the aiming stakes were in the proper alignment in his optical sight. The tube was then at the correct position to fire the round.

During the time that the company was standing down and as the first 11C replacements were arriving, Rich and I were working with the two surviving members of the platoon, Halpin (I cannot remember his first name) and Jim Bevard. They were both in the FDC (Fire Direction Center) squad, so they would give us the data from practice fire missions and we would practice putting them into our gun sights. We did this for a couple of days, but Rich and I really needed crews to start practicing moving our guns around and making the final adjustments on the bipod legs to finish the gun setup.

So early on we asked gun crews from Bravo, Charlie or Delta Companies' mortar platoons to help us practice. Usually one crew from two different companies would come over and help us out. The makeup of their platoons was similar to ours, consisting of 11 Charlies and 11 Bravos, most of whom had been on-line and had been rewarded and assigned to the mortars. At first they were very uncomfortable around us. We were the remnants of the unthinkable nightmare, and they simply didn't know how to act around us. However, their discomfort quickly disappeared. All of these borrowed crew members helped Rich and me improve our gunner skills as our own platoon's replacements trickled in. These replacements were fresh 11 Charlies, straight from stateside training, so their learning curve was not as steep as Rich's and mine. We soon said goodbye to our fellow Battalion mortar men.

CHAPTER 41

LICKING OUR WOUNDS IN SONG BE

Meanwhile, across the basecamp, the other men of Alpha Company were also receiving replacements and were training as they organized into some kind of field-ready company. My assistant gunner Jimmy White took over my M60 gun and a volunteer from the platoon was made Assistant Gunner. So with the addition of a new ammo bearer, my old gun was in good hands. The other gun crew in Mike Platoon was intact, but the two machine gun crews in each of Lima and November Platoons were made up of some new men. New medics were assigned to each platoon as well as new platoon leaders. Mike platoon had some experienced men in each skill position who became important trainers for the incoming replacements. The survivors from Lima and November Platoons, along with Mike Platoon survivors, would go out on day patrols as training missions for the newbies. In the beginning, their nights were spent back at Quan Loi. Later, practicing ambushes was introduced, and then at some point they stayed outside the wire at night for some actual ambushes. The one thing that was never practiced was an aerial insertion using helicopters; aerial insertions would come later.

Slowly but surely, the different parts of Alpha Company were making progress on the basic skills required to survive in the field. A couple of weeks after the company rebuilding began, Battalion assigned our company, including the mortars, to Song Be to continue our training. Song Be was a small outpost, about 100 yards in diameter, built around a 105 Howitzer battery. Earlier in the year when we had worked out of Song Be, the entire battalion had moved its headquarters there, and the four rifle companies had rotated in and out of the bunker line. Three of the four companies would be out patrolling and ambushing and the fourth one would be on the bunker line protecting the battalion headquarters and the artillery. So each company would be out in the bush for 15 days, which was about average. Then they would come in for five days of bunker duty and a few daytime practice patrols. Even though we would have daytime patrols, bunker duty was nice duty.

We discovered several other benefits of the Song Be location. One, the battalion had a kitchen there so we had hot chow for most meals. Two, we were able to receive mail with packages. Three, we could shower every day. And four, it was the only time that our company mortars would be located close to the rifle platoons. Whenever a company had the bunker line duty at Song Be, their own mortars would leave Quan Loi and join them at Song Be. The mortars were used for perimeter security and occasionally for fire support for the units in the field. The benefit was that during these bunker line days a person could go visit an old friend who had transferred to mortars; at Quan Loi, the mortar platoon was too far away for visits.

While the company was rebuilding at Song Be, the rifle platoons continued to do patrols and ambushes, but in a more controlled and open area, while we continued to practice our mortar skills in the basecamp. Eventually we started firing live rounds three or four times a day during H and I (Harassment and Interdiction) Missions. H and I Missions were missions during which we would randomly fire rounds at pre-selected targets or areas such as clearings from which the enemy had previously launched rockets or mortars. Each of these fire missions was a live-fire practice for us. The one thing that we were never allowed to do during training was to fire live rounds when Song Be had incoming (enemy mortar or missile attacks). These were called counter-fire missions. Song Be received rocket or mortar attacks almost daily. Normally, when the incoming would start, the 105 howitzers and the local mortars (us) would fire two or three rounds at a number of pre-selected areas that incoming had originated from before. We would continue to fire until all targets on the list had been engaged. It was a bit nerve-racking because we were in the open while the incoming was landing around the compound. However, during training, with our lack of experience and the added tension of incoming, they didn't trust us to be accurate until our skills were much more developed, which was probably very wise.

At some point, the company was deemed Combat Ready, and all of the superstitious old combat vets were nervous as hell. We all knew that there were too many greenies in the company, but there were no other options. The piper would be paid. That also meant that I would start firing counter-fire missions.

On the very first day that we were Combat Ready, we got our usual incoming, and I had to jump into my gun position and start firing our counter-fire mission. I was so focused on my new job that I don't even remember if it was day or night. I was aware that the enemy rounds were walking my way; I would feel the thump and then hear the splash. They were 70 yards away, then 50 yards and still coming, still no problem. Then a soft thump and a crackled splash—oh-oh, it hit something. Keep focused, keep focused! Then all of a sudden heads of lettuce, raw meat, carrots, large pieces of Styrofoam and chunks of plywood started to rain down on us. The enemy had made a direct hit on the walk-in cooler at the battalion kitchen. All of the men in the two mortar rings started laughing uncontrollably as we were still firing our counter-fire rounds. No one else in camp knew about it because they were in their bunkers. One or two more enemy rounds came in and then stopped, as we continued to laugh and finish our assigned mission. Men started coming out of their bunkers and wondered what the hell we were laughing about and then joined us in laughter as they discovered the food scattered all around the area.

Across an open area, the men from the 105 battery were whooping and hollering and congratulating us for having completed our first counter-fire mission. They started coming over as they heard everyone laughing and joined in the fun. The only ones not having a good time were the cooks, who immediately understood that they were going to have to salvage as much of the food as possible and cook it all up to keep it from spoiling.

We ate well for the next couple of days, as the cooks were trying to use as much food as possible until the new cooler arrived. Welcome to mortars, Doug!

CHAPTER 42

MIKE PLATOON GETS BLOODIED AGAIN

The rifle platoons were now battle ready and were sent out on search and destroy missions. Mike Platoon was still the go-to platoon. Even though Mike platoon no longer had SSG. Wright, they had the highest number of survivors of the three platoons. For the first several eagle flights (aerial insertions), Mike led the way. It was logical that they should, and everything went well for the first couple of times.

Then on the third or fourth mission, for some reason unknown to the grunts, the 105 battery did not prep the LZ. Prior to that day, the 105 battery would always fire 10 to 20 rounds into and around any LZ before we landed. The purpose was to scatter any enemy in the area or to discourage any organized enemy resistance in the LZ. Most of the old timers thought it was a battalion, brigade or division policy to always prep an LZ, but for some reason that morning, the artillery did not receive orders and the LZ was not prepped.

Mike Platoon was the lead platoon and got on the choppers for the first wave in. They took off for a short ride, and just as they were about to disembark from their choppers, all hell broke loose. The LZ was a two-sided trap or ambush. The platoon was on the ground but the fire at the choppers was fierce. Somehow all of the choppers managed to fly away. There were numerous enemy machine guns and automatic assault guns ripping into Mike platoon. The most frightening and unusual weapon was a

51-caliber machine gun. That gun is a huge weapon and was usually used against hard targets. It was seldom used as an anti-personnel weapon. That weapon was a very serious and frightening development because it put Mike platoon as well as aircraft and light armor in jeopardy.

I was back in Song Be in mortars, and I was going crazy. It was within five or six miles of our base, and we all could hear the firefight. Rich and I heard and recognized the sound of the 51-caliber gun. We couldn't believe it because we had never encountered it in our missions in the bush. We just knew Mike was getting chewed up. We watched the men from the 105 Howitzers run to their guns and get ready for a close support fire mission. A bit later, they started to fire single rounds as someone in Mike Platoon radioed in the adjustments to help place the rounds where they were needed.

The air strip was just outside the wire and was probably only 100 yards from our position. We heard the choppers come back and load up the next wave to go reinforce Mike. A couple of wounded were helped off the choppers, and then the choppers took off with the second wave of men. The sounds of the firefight were ebbing and flowing as each side was maneuvering for an advantage. The choppers didn't come back on time, so we all guessed that the LZ was so hot that they couldn't get back in and they were looking for another spot to get the second wave on the ground. Once the rest of the company was on the ground, they would hump over and try to relieve the first wave of guys from Mike Platoon.

The wounded were brought from the airstrip and back to our area. They had gotten a quick patch from the medic that was still on the tarmac and were stable enough to wait for a later medevac chopper. I recognized one of the wounded as the new ammo bearer from my gun. I didn't know his name, but I asked him what had happened and whether Jimmy White and his assistant were OK. He said that he (the ammo bearer) had been hit twice in the leg as he jumped out of the chopper and that Jimmy had told him to drop his ammo and jump back on the chopper. He said that as he left, both Jimmy and his assistant were OK and running away from the choppers.

Rich and I kept listening to the sounds of the firefight and could tell that it was a tough one. We could distinguish the unique sound of each weapon since an AK sounds different from an M16 or M60 or the big 51 caliber machine gun. We could tell that one or two helicopter gunships had arrived and that was good. Now the firefight seemed to slow down a bit with the air support, but the 51 just didn't stop—not good. We kept saying to each other that the 51 must be dug in and maybe even had some overhead protection. Our guys needed to spot that gun and fire some rockets from the gunship to take it out.

Meanwhile the rest of the company had landed four or five kilometers away in another clearing, but that was a long way away from Mike, which meant that it would be at least an hour or more before Mike got any help. Rich and I got an extra radio from somewhere and were listening to the Company net (the radio talk between Mike's point squad, the platoon sergeant and the CO). On and on the firefight went. Rich and I were really anxious because this was the first firefight that our old platoon had been in since we left them, and these were our best friends. Mike Platoon was in a bad firefight, and we knew that more than half of those guys were green. However, the radio talk told us that they were doing OK and were not sustaining heavy losses. Yet, that damned 51 just kept firing.

The firefight went on for more than an hour, but it did eventually taper off a bit and then the 51 stopped firing. A platoon of armored infantry from our sister battalion, the 2nd of the 2nd Infantry (we were the 1st of the 2nd Infantry), had arrived and rolled up the enemy. An armored platoon is four or five M113 APCs (armored personnel carriers) that usually have two or three mounted machine guns on each APC and can overrun an enemy position pretty quickly.

So Mike Platoon finally got rescued after a long firefight. The mechanized platoon then set up a secure perimeter and Mike got to stand down, take care of their casualties and call in some Medevacs. Next they took an inventory of their combat equipment. A bit later the rest of Alpha Company arrived and took over security, thanked the mechanized platoon and bid them a thanks-filled good bye.

I recall this story and include it here because I remember the intense guilt of survival that Rich and I experienced that day and in ensuing days. We were at once incredibly relieved that we had not been in that tough firefight; after all we were living a new life that we had been dreaming, hoping and praying about for months. We were also feeling incredibly guilty about not being out there contributing our honed skills in getting everybody home. The only rule that the grunts of the draft infantry lived by was that we all had to contribute our best to get everybody home, because there was absolutely nothing else we could rely on other than each other. Mike Platoon had been bloodied and Rich and I felt like shit. Little did we know that the guilt of survival would be a lifelong companion.

CHAPTER 43

RE-UPPING

I remember two different times, when we had heavy losses that, some men would lose their nerve and reenlist (re-upping) in the army, in order to be assigned a different job and get off-line. The army would make the person enlist for three years and offer only one choice for a new job, a helicopter door gunner. Even though that job was no free pass to safety, it was definitely a better job than being in the infantry. We worked 24/7, whereas they spent many nights in bed with sheets, and they had hot chow all of the time. We had two men re-up after the four days that we were badly chewed up, and one soldier re-upped after another tough time. As much as everyone hated our infantry life, we were all counting our days until we went home, and for all of us it was within a year. The idea that we would sign up for three more years in the army was just intolerable. We all hated the army more than we hated our life on-line.

PART 7

DAU TIENG

CHAPTER 44

WORKING MORTARS IN DAU TIENG

In late spring of 1969, the United States started to wind down the war by reducing the number of troops in Vietnam. On April 30, 1969, the troop strength in Vietnam had reached the all-time high-water mark of 543,482 soldiers. By late summer, they started to send Infantry units back to the States. In my part of the country along the Cambodian Border, the 25th Infantry Division began shifting the AOs of some of their units in preparation of the one year process of deploying back to their home base in Hawaii. Part of their AO was to our south along the Cambodian Border. That shift of the 25th Division started a whole series of changing AO's for the remaining Infantry units along the Cambodian Border. This caused the 1st Infantry Division to move south by reallocating some of our units (my 1st Brigade) to the south. North of us, the 1st Cavalry Division likewise shifted units south to cover some of our former AO. Sometime in late September or early October, I moved south with the 1st brigade of the 1st Division to the Dau Tieng basecamp.

The Dau Tieng basecamp was built around yet another cluster of early century French rubber plantation owners' and managers' beautiful Art Deco mansions. This enclave too had been set up to maintain a bit of French Society in the interior of colonial Vietnam. Among the amenities that these rural enclaves (including Lai Khe and Quan Loi) usually had was a Water Polo swimming pool. A Water Polo pool does not have a

Enos, Ikehera, Reveria and Lovejoy filling sandbags with the above-ground three-meter pool in the background.

shallow area in the pool but is about three meters (around ten feet) deep throughout the pool. I'm sure that it provided years of refreshing entertainment and socializing for all of the colonists. The noteworthy fact about the Dau Tieng pool was that, unlike the other pools that I saw in Vietnam which were built into the ground, the Dau Tieng pool was completely above ground.

The pool was seldom used. I only swam in it once, and all I remember is how chlorinated it was. I could only stand to be in it for a few minutes. When I got out I had crystals of chlorine form on my eyelashes, and I itched so badly that I had to sneak into some unit's showers and take a cold shower to rinse off the chlorine.

When we arrived in Dau Tieng, we were trucked to the area at which we were to set up our mortars. We off-loaded our mortar and personal gear. Next we laid out the exact locations of the two gun rings and the FDC (Fire Direction Control). The FDC needed to be a small, room-sized bunker with room for three or four men to work at a table with several radios together at one end of the table. I think we found an old abandoned bunker that we refurbished because I can't remember building the FDC. We then laid out and built the gun rings so that they would be within shouting distance from the FDC entrance.

Kurtz, Enos, Smith and Bevard beginning to build one of our gun rings. Notice the wood floor in the ammo bunker to keep the ammo dry.

Sometime later, a big army dump truck showed up and dumped a couple piles of sand and a bunch of empty sandbags. All of us just groaned and started to fill them up.

A gun ring was a 15- to 18-foot circle of sandbags that was two feet thick and 30 to 32 inches high. This provided minimal protection from shrapnel and small arms fire for the gun crew. At one end of the ring a square bump-out was formed as the ammo bunker. This bunker was open to the ring and was made of sandbagged walls and roof, each two feet thick.

We started to lay sandbags around the circle and then we would pound them flat and dense. Around and around we positioned them in place and pounded the hell out of them. We took shifts laying them, which wore out our backs, and beating them, which blistered our hands. There were no gloves in sight. Then a day and a half later a truck arrived and we unloaded a basic load of ammo that came from the base ammo dump. We were now in business and our business was mostly perimeter defense. Since there were several mortar units located in Dau Tieng, each unit had an assigned sector of the perimeter.

Over the next few days, we started plotting predetermined target areas along our sector. These were logged in the FDC so that if the basecamp was attacked in our sector, we would be able to initiate our fire missions very quickly. These targets were places where the terrain was unusual, like a draw or a spot where the fence was not as secure. These conditions could give an advantage to an enemy force preparing for a nighttime attack.

We now settled into a routine of continuous radio monitoring and practicing dry fire missions. Once again I was on an ironclad 24/7 schedule; we were shorthanded, and we were all needed every minute so we could provide our lethal services. Several times a week we would be given a fire mission from our artillery handlers, and we would practice live fire missions. At nights, we were often radioed H and I (harassment and interdiction) missions during which we directed live rounds into areas from which enemy mortars and rockets had been launched in recent months. These fire missions were rotated among all of the mortar and artillery units in the basecamp.

This routine continued until our new company commander found a 60mm mortar tube and some ammo for it. Our mortars were 81mm and were much larger, heavier and more powerful than the 60. The 60 tubes were not used by the US Army infantry divisions at that time but had been designated as surplus and given to the Vietnamese Army. We could no longer draw ammo or parts from our supply system for the 60mm mortar. The CO got the stupid idea that, with our mortar platoon strength of 15 or so men, we had enough men to also be able to hump the 60 tube in the field. To send four or five men out in the bush would make us very short-handed in our platoon and make it very difficult, or most likely impossible, to accomplish a long-lasting fire mission; we wouldn't have enough men to plot the many adjustments and prepare and fire the required rounds for an extended period of time.

Our CO didn't have a clue of these facts any more than he understood why the 81 mortars were not taken into the field. Our AO had terrain and over-cover that made firing mortars impossible most of the time. Therefore the rifle platoons seldom were operating in the open. Duh!!!!!!

Rich and I were the only men in the platoon that had humped in the field and we were both gunners, so we knew we would be in the rotation for humping the damn thing. The whole platoon practiced calculating solutions and dry firing missions on the new 60mm mortar. Rich and I finally persuaded the platoon sergeant to send out a team of the new guys for the first trip. However, we couldn't change his mind about not using us in the rotation. So we knew that something had to be done to stop the stupidity of this 60mm mortar.

So out into the bush did our new brave, naïve, wide-eyed mortar men march with the little 60mm. In two and a half or three weeks they came back in, and they had had their asses whipped. Rich and I now had four more allies to our cause of foiling the 60. Rich and I were very sweet and sympathetic to their pain and exhaustion, and we volunteered to clean the tube for them while they cleaned up and rested.

Since there was no cleaning equipment for this tube, we found a rod that could be used, some appropriate cleaning solvent and several nice clean rags. We then swabbed the tube with solvent and then wrapped the rag around the rod preparing to run it in the tube for the final cleaning. It was at this point that we added a very special and unseen "tool" that we had found in our motor pool scrap pile. It was a nice cylinder of solid steel that would fit at the end of the rod, allow a towel to be wrapped around it and slide perfectly down the tube without scratching the sides. We were pretty certain that this special "tool" would accomplish our special need of destroying the tube. When we

Most of the men of Alpha Company's Mortar Platoon

slammed the rod down the tube our special "tool" hit the firing pin located at the bottom center of the tube and severely bent it.

As a mortar round is dropped down the tube, the firing pin is used to ignite the primer on the mortar round exactly the same way the firing pin does on a common gun. A bent firing pin does not possess the proper and critical position to fire the primer on the round. Oh, my gosh! After we threw away our special "tool," Rich and I "felt just awful" that the firing pin was bent. We appropriately hung our heads and reported to our platoon sergeant that we thought that our jerry-rigged cleaning tool kit might have bent the pin and that he needed to order a replacement. We knew damn well that there would be no replacement; the weapon wasn't in OUR army's inventory. So much for the stupidity of humping a 60mm mortar in the bush. Dumb ass CO!

CHAPTER 45

TO ANOTHER NEW JOB I GO

At some point during our time in Dau Tieng, I was told that they wanted me to transfer into the FDC and therefore leave the gunner's job. I think part of the reason was that they wanted me, as a sergeant, to be more formally the second in command of the platoon, and they wanted me in the FDC bunker. The FDC, or Fire Direction Center, is comprised of men who use maps and plotting/calculating devices to acquire the data that is used by the gunner in his gun sight to set the proper angle for the gun tube. So once again I started to retrain myself. I had to learn how to operate the radios, how to read maps much better and how to locate and update the necessary friendly positions as well as the locations of the desired fire missions.

I met this change with conflicting views. I enjoyed being outside with the gun and the crew. We worked together well and enjoyed each other's company. We had a good healthy competition with Rich's crew which made us work better and become a bit closer. All of the required tasks for the gun were performed outside, whereas the men in the FDC spent all of their time in the FDC bunker and living in an old bunker was very dismal. I changed over to the FDC, but I was going to miss working the crew and the gun.

In our basic load of ammo, we stocked three different types of mortar rounds. High Explosive (HE) comprised the largest number of rounds in our pits. These were used as antipersonnel

Mike Humlicek visiting Rich Lovejoy and me at mortars

rounds and for destroying hard targets. The next most numerous type of round was the Illumination Round (ILLUM). It was used to light up an area for better visibility. Using it to illuminate bunker lines was a very common practice. The final type of round in our inventory was the White Phosphorus (WP) round. White Phosphorus was a molten metal so hot that it would melt through steel. It was used to create a smoke screen, to destroy hard targets, start fires and as the ultimate antipersonnel weapon. The enemy was absolutely terrified of what we flippantly called Willy Peter or Wilson Picket. We too were afraid of it and were very happy that the enemy did not use it against us, at least not in this AO.

WP has been banned as an antipersonnel weapon, as has napalm, by a number of Treaties to which the U.S. has been a party. However, it allegedly was used against troops in several operations in Iraq. The confusion surrounding these and other charges is that WP is not banned for use as a smoke screen, marker round or as an incendiary device so it is in the inventory of many mortar and artillery batteries. This allows use in areas in which people are burned either intentionally or by accident. I can't remember ever using it in any of our fire missions against people, not that I would have hesitated in the slightest if it was needed.

One night we received a call from the arty net (our radio contact) to stand by because of activity in and around our perimeter sector. Soon all of the men were ready at their guns and FDC positions and were prepared to commence a fire mission. In a short time, we received our first mission for illumination. That was the beginning of about a four-hour mission.

The illumination of our sector confirmed that there was a massing of enemy troops in our sector. With the illumination the surprise factor was gone and the NVA force began its attack on the perimeter. Since it was our sector, we switched to firing High Explosive rounds, and another mortar platoon took over the illumination rounds. We fired pretty steadily for over an hour; then we slowed down a bit as our rounds were used to chase groups who had been identified as trying to withdraw. Finally, we slowed down to an H and I routine across our entire sector after the NVA were not seen in the area.

Since we had illumination from the beginning of this attack the NVA were not able to retrieve their dead and the next day an infantry unit swept our sector and reported a body count of 17 NVA. Of all of the days I had spent in the field with my machine gun, ironically, this is the largest head count that I ever had a direct hand in, and I never saw a single face, pair of eyes, enemy muzzle flash or twisted, grisly body to confront. I wonder how pilots, artillery men and drone-masters deal with their kills, but I will say that this kill certainly was a lot easier on me than a number of others that occurred when I was out in the field.

CHAPTER 46

A LOT OF STRIPES AND NO BRAINS

"OK, Alpha Company Mortars, pack up!" Oh shit, a new adventure. "Pack your tubes, radios and plotting boards and leave the rest of your shit here. You'll be back in less than a week. A truck will be here in 30 minutes." Damn! We packed up and jumped onto a truck and were driven to the airstrip where we met up with our company. For Rich and me, it was a nice treat to see some of our friends from Mike platoon. After some time, two Shithooks flew in, and we and one of the rifle platoons were ordered into the two choppers. Top joined us in our chopper and the CO jumped in the other chopper.

I have no idea where we went, but we flew for nearly an hour, which was a long time for us to fly in a Shithook. My guess was that we were close to but not in Saigon. The terrain was open, a bit hilly and had a sparse but evenly-distributed population. It reminded me of an area of small agricultural plots. I can't remember where we landed, but I think maybe it was on a road. The two choppers left to get the rest of the company. We didn't stay to secure the area but started to walk away from the road. It must have been a pretty safe area, at least during daylight, to land two expensive Chinooks without security. We humped for less than an hour and stopped on the top of a small hill somewhat away from any settlements and with two large piles of new sandbags.

Now things were coming into focus. We were going to build a firebase. A firebase is a small fortified camp with some kind of fire support unit in the middle of the camp. A firebase of this size was either for a battery of 105mm howitzers or a small bore mortar platoon. So the old man (CO) and First Sergeant started to lay out the base. Since the function of the base was to protect a fire support unit, the location of our fire rings was assigned early. They laid out two rings and told us to start building the fire rings for mortars. We started to build and it was nice because at first no one else was after any tools or sandbags. We had a great start on both rings and we were soon working on the FDC bunker.

The layout of the fire base seemed strange to us because it was too small (too few bunkers) for an American-sized company and soon the buzz around the base was that we were making a fire base for the ARVNs (Army of the Republic of Vietnam). This did not please us. Why couldn't they make their own? Three hours later the rest of the company arrived and we all worked at making all of the bunkers for the basecamp. As the afternoon was waning the CO told us to set up our tubes and start calculating perimeter defensive plots (predetermined areas where we would fire our mortars outside the perimeter in case of an attack that night).

This baseplate needs to be set with a charge (Courtesy http://publicdomainvectors.org.)

We in the FDC started to do our calculations, and the gun crews set up the guns and placed the aiming posts that they would use with their sights. The bottom end of a mortar is fastened to a circular metal piece called the baseplate, which, when set into the ground, keeps the mortar from drifting sideways while firing rounds. The photo (right) shows a mortar tube and baseplate; the photo shows the baseplate on top of the ground without the bottom ridges "set." After the setup of the gun, the baseplate must be settled or "set" into the soil. The plate is set into the ground by firing a high charged round very close to straight up in the air so that the recoil would force the baseplate straight down. After the baseplate is set, then the final adjustments to the gun's sighting system are made, since that one round caused the baseplate to move down four or more inches. With these final adjustments to the sighting rods, the tube is now ready for a mission. Each round fired now will force the baseplate to move very little.

We calculated a plot that placed the round's explosion as close to the basecamp as safely possible. This action causes the angle of the tube to be as close to vertical as feasible and therefore push the plate straight down. Normally we would use a small powder charge for a target this close-in and therefore the round would come down in a short time. However, since the purpose of this round was to settle the baseplate we determined the largest charge that we could use for our close target. Since this was a very small base we chose a very close-in target and therefore the tube was very, very vertical.

We then yelled that we were going to fire and nobody paid a bit of attention. "Fire in the hole!" and the assistant gunner dropped the round in the tube, and there was a nice loud mortar report. The baseplate settled in about four or so inches as was intended, and with the settlement of the tube, it became almost perfectly vertical. "Oh, my God, the round went straight up," shouted the lifer First Sergeant as he started scurrying around looking for cover. This of course caused immediate panic among the entire company as everyone was reacting to the dumb ass's message.

Actually, the mortar round leaves the tube at the original angle, and the force that settles the baseplate is the recoil of the round leaving the tube. The gun tube is THEN naturally settled into a more vertical position than when the round left the tube. The Lifer First Sergeant was now running around yelling as our entire mortar platoon was calmly going about its work. At some point, he noticed that we were calm and he must have remembered a part of a class he took about mortars and realized that he had just made not only a huge mistake but also a fool of himself. He calmed down and tried to act cool. A round that has a maximum charge and is sent in a vertical trajectory takes a long, long time to come back down to explode or "splash." This whole time the company was observing and thinking about what a dufus we had for a First Sergeant. Pretty soon the round came down and splashed about a hundred yards outside the perimeter right where it was supposed to. From that day forward, the First Sergeant never recovered the loss of respect of many of the men because of those few moments of panic and stupidity.

CHAPTER 47

MY CHANCE AT HEAVEN

One day out of the blue towards the end of my tour, our great company clerk came over and told me that he had secured a three-day pass for me. Bless his heart; I didn't even know there was such a thing as a three-day pass in Nam. I should have known, though, because I'm sure all the rear echelon jerks had them. The pass was for Vung Tau, an old colonial French beach resort town on the South China Sea. I didn't know anything about Vung Tau, but I certainly was going to go. The only word of warning from the clerk was to be wary of "girls of Vung Tau" since they were not as medically-controlled or overseen as the girls of Bangkok and Hong Kong.

Early the next day, I followed his instructions and went over to the company headquarters to check in my M16, and then I walked over to the Dau Tieng airstrip to catch a damn C-7 Caribou flight to Di An. While there, I met a soldier from Charlie Company with a pass too. We flew down to Di An and were there by 9:00 a.m. We off loaded and were told to be back at the strip at 4:30 p.m. for the flight to Vung Tau. We thought, "As late as 4:30! No way—we weren't going to spend one of our precious three days waiting for a plane ride." Neither one of us had a map or knew where Vung Tau was so we started to ask around to see if anyone knew anything about Vung Tau. The most common answer we got was that it was down the road to the south. Both of us had fewer than sixty days left in-country, and we found ourselves standing at the front gate of Di An. Di An to us seemed like stateside; hardly anything happens in and around Di An. Standing at the gate we started to process all we knew about Vung Tau and the countryside to the south. We knew that the further a person went north from here, the more dangerous it got; therefore, we figured that the further south we went it probably would get safer.

So, fueled by the collective impatience of being in the infantry and not getting to do anything fun for a year, we made the decision to walk out the front gate of Di An unarmed, stick out our thumb and hitch a ride to Vung Tau. About 30 seconds later, the first US Army deuce and a half truck (2 ½ ton) pulled over. We asked if he was headed for Vung Tau. He replied with a smile that he was heading south towards it and to hop in. We gladly jumped in back. "Yup," we thought, "we have made the right decision—piece of cake!"

We stretched out and smugly dozed off. Sometime later the truck stopped, and the driver said he was turning off the highway. He told us to get out but not to worry because another truck would most likely be along soon. Sure enough, a few minutes later several trucks came along and stopped. We jumped in the back of one and were again on our way.

This pattern continued all morning and into the afternoon, but the time between the trucks became longer. We no longer felt smug but instead were starting to feel a bit exposed. As we got off the last US truck, they told us that we were now entering the Australian Army's AO and by the way, "Don't let the MPs catch you out of the American AO." Oh shit! We sat down and waited for our first Aussie truck.

In a bit, a deuce and a half came along and sure enough it was an Aussie-driven truck. They were glad to meet us and told us to jump in. We were up front in this truck, and we found out that we were indeed traveling towards Vung Tau but that he was going to be turning off way short of the city. He assured us that there should be plenty of traffic to help us continue our trek. So in the middle of the afternoon, we rode with several different Aussies on our way to what now was starting to feel like the Emerald City. Our last Aussie told us that he was turning off the highway to go to a basecamp and that we were now entering the

Thailand Army's AO. We were then realizing that we definitely should have taken the 4:30 flight; we would have been there by this time.

We were getting a bit spooked now. This was the first time in eleven months that we were not armed to the teeth, and frankly, we were feeling extremely undressed. Instead of being loaded down with multiple weapons, we were sitting by the side of the road, defenseless and waiting for something to happen. In a few minutes, another deuce and a half, this time with Thai Army markings, pulled up and stopped. "VUNG TAU? VUNG TAU?" we shouted. Apparently, we were hoping the volume would somehow translate our English into Thai. They smiled and nodded their heads yes, yes enthusiastically and helped us into the back of the truck. There were about ten Thai soldiers and the two of us in the back and we were all smiles as we traded cigarettes and became great friends. "Maybe the situation isn't as bad as we were thinking," we hoped. In about a half hour the truck pulled into a small town and parked at the town square. As soon as the wheels stopped, every last one of them jumped out of the truck and disappeared into the crowd.

The guy from Charlie and I looked at each other and wondered if this trip could get any more screwed up. We decide to wait for a few minutes in the truck and see what developed. Truthfully there wasn't any other choice since we were in a village that was not in the American AO. On the other hand, nobody was paying much attention to us. After about 10 or 15 minutes, as if on cue, they all showed up and jumped into the truck and we drove out of the village. We were on the road again, and at this stage that was the best we could hope for.

The deuce and a half with its smiling cross-cultural load of merry soldiers continued to roll south but it was getting to be early evening now. The one thing we knew was that we didn't want to spend the night unarmed, outdoors and outside the American AO, especially after hundreds of people had seen us. Again we asked ourselves, "Could this trip get any more screwed up?" We didn't have long to wait for an answer. It could.

The truck came to a halt in the middle of nowhere and everybody smiled and pointed for us to get out. Oh shit! So we jumped down, smiled and backed away from the truck. We really felt naked now. Simultaneously they all waved at us, made a sharp right turn off the road into nowhere and drove out of sight. We now knew that we were in trouble. So we started to walk quickly down the road, trying to put some miles away from the point where we had been dropped off by the Thais.

Soon we heard the sound of a diesel engine approaching us from behind and we turned around, expecting to see a military vehicle, but instead we saw a civilian bus approaching us. By this time we were hoping this was good news. We waved the bus down and we again yelled with hope, "VUNG TAU? VUNG TAU?" The driver shook his head. "Oh shit," we thought, and our hearts sank. But then he smiled and pointed to his watch, pointed specifically to the minute hand and then pointed to a half hour later. He did this several times while repeating the words Vung Tau. Was he telling us that a bus to Vung Tau was 30 minutes behind him? Could we rally our fading hopes one more time? We smiled broadly and waved to him as he drove away.

Light was fading now, and we started to walk fast again to put distance between ourselves and our last contact with civilians. We were making plans to walk on the road as far and fast as we could and then find a hiding place off the road after dark. We were humping fast when we heard another diesel engine. Thank God there was enough light to distinguish that it was a bus. A few minutes later, we would have been too afraid to flag down a pair of headlights. As the bus approached, we saw a sign in the window that listed several towns including Vung Tau. Halleluiah! Halleluiah! We hailed him to stop and stepped into the bus to ask the driver the cost for us to ride to Vung Tau. Whatever it was, we eagerly paid, knowing we had just paid four or five times the actual price. Finally we were going to make it to Vung Tau, our Emerald City.

It was dark now and we were cruising along, thinking that this must be a pretty safe area in which to be driving an hour after dark. We could see the lights of a large town ahead and soon we were slowing down at a check point at the edge of the town. Shit! We could see American and Vietnamese MPs at the road block. We knew one thing for sure—we absolutely, positively could not get caught in this civilian bus coming in out of the countryside from a non-American AO. We would definitely be screwed. It was too late to jump off the bus so we did the next best thing—we scrunched down among the people and small livestock and bet on the MP's boredom and incompetence to pull us through. It worked. One of them stepped onto the bus, looked around for a couple of seconds (we didn't know which one since we were busy making ourselves very small), and in a very short time, we were rolling into town.

As soon as we got a few miles into the town, we jumped off the bus and started walking. Soon we found a GI, and we asked him where the American check-in for our passes was so that we could check in. We reported in about six hours late, and we were grilled about where we had been. They wondered why we hadn't taken the military bus from the airstrip to the check-in location. "Don't you know that we could send you back to your unit tomorrow?" We just acted a bit drunk (we did have alcohol breath since we bought some form of booze the moment we got off the bus) and gave them the "we're in the infantry and we don't give a shit about anything" look, and we toughed our way through the check-in.

We got the list of MP-approved hotels, checked into one of them, got something to eat and got drunk. The next morning we ate breakfast and asked some GIs where to go shopping for some cheap clothes for the day, since we would be throwing them away the next morning when we went back. We then grabbed a pedicab, stopped at one or two shops for some clothes and a swimming suit and headed for the beach.

We went to a beautiful beach filled with hundreds of GIs. Three days ago, my new friend and I hadn't even known three-day passes existed in Nam. Now we saw hundreds of GIs on this beach, which meant that there were thousands in Vung Tau. Life in-country can be pretty good if one gets the right assignment, we thought. One more kick in the groin for the infantry.

The city and beach's setting was of declining colonial glamor. The white sandy shoreline was lined with fading fifty year old hotels and between and around them were all sorts of stalls and shacks selling anything or everything to the GIs. We got into our swimming suits somewhere, stuffed our money in our suits and ran into the South China Sea. Wow, was this going to be great!

We had been standing chest-deep in the water for about two or three minutes when a couple of turds floated between us. We just stood there for a second, then turned and walked out of the water, muttering and cursing about revolting luck. We walked into a hotel, changed into our clothes, threw away our swimming suits and went into the hotel bar.

I only have one other memory of that three-day "excursion"—my purchase of a fine tailored suit. As near as I can recall, I was on my way to the restroom in the lower concourse level of the hotel when I passed a tailor shop. I remember that the tailor was East Indian and that I had two or three fittings over the course of the day. I recall also that I gave them my address in Iowa for them to ship it home. When I got back to the states, I could wear that suit for about two months and then I never could get into it again. That evening we took a pedicab back to our hotel and crashed.

The next day the hotel staff woke us up in time to get to the military airstrip on time for our flight back to Di An. By 3 o'clock that afternoon we were back in Dau Tieng, and I was back into the grind of monitoring the radios 24/7 again. My only three-day pass was a case study of stupidity, impatience and life in the third world, but nothing about having fun.

CHAPTER 48

A MAGNIFICENT SCHEME

Late in October we started hearing rumors about big changes in our battalion's mortars. Rich and I were concerned because we were getting pretty "short" (closing in on 30 days left in our tour). We had a reasonably safe job now and we didn't want any changes taking place. Early November brought the big announcement:

ALL FOUR OF THE 1ST BATTALION 2ND INFANTRY MORTAR PLATOONS WILL MERGE INTO A SINGLE MEGA 81mm MORTAR UNIT!

"Wow! What a fabulous idea! Boy, oh boy, will that ever make a difference! We must have a new brilliant Battalion Commander to lead us ever forward," thought all of us old timers. In other words, "What a crock of shit this new idea was."

All we knew early on was that our mission and troop strength wouldn't change. Each company would still have the same perimeter sector of responsibility and the same H and I assignments, so what was the point? Shortly all four company mortar platoons met face to face and were told to shut up and sit down so that the magnificent scheme could be unveiled unto us.

The plan was that, collectively, we were going to abandon six of the eight mortar rings and ammo storage bunkers, as well as all four of the FDC bunkers. We would move those assets to the area near the remaining intact two rings and build six new rings and ammo bunkers and a new supersized FDC bunker. It all sounded like a bunch of hard sand bagging work to us. Shit.

As for the assigned personnel, they took the entire pool of men and separated us into 4 groups: Group 1) all men with rank of E-4 and below who had more than 30 days left in-country, 2) all NCOs (non-commissioned officers or sergeants) E-5 or E-6 with more than 30 days left in-country, 3) all men E-4 and below with fewer than 30 days left and 4) all NCOs with fewer than 30 days left.

The strategy was that anyone with fewer than 30 days left wasn't worth training or bothering with. Since our platoon had been wiped out earlier, Rich and I were the only people from A Company mortars with fewer than 30 days left to serve in-country; not surprisingly, Rich and I couldn't have agreed more with the strategy. So that morning everyone with more than thirty days left got trucked off together and started to build the new mortar complex and train together as a single, larger unit. Except for Rich, I never saw any of my mortar buddies again.

Meanwhile, we short-timers were pulled aside and informed that from now on we were on permanent detail duty. Details were shit jobs that are assigned to soldiers to keep them busy – busy work. We formed into several groups, with one sergeant (like me) in charge of two or three E-4s. For the first day's detail, we were all told to go to the battalion motor pool and sign out a deuce and a half vehicle and a number of portable hand pumps from our battalion supply. One of the E-5s had a truck driver's license, and he drove us all to the POL (petroleum, oil, lubricants) which was basically the base fuel dump.

We took a 55 gallon drum and filled it with 45 gallons of diesel fuel and ten gallons of Mogas (military gasoline) and then drove to a designated section of the perimeter. We tipped the drum on its side and started to fill the hand pumps with this concoction and started spraying it on the weeds and brush that were growing on and between the concertina wire rolls. This vegetation was hindering the view from the bunkers of the front firing fields of the bunkers.

About 20 gallons of the mixture was sprayed onto about 40 or 50 yards of brush at which point we sergeants thought we should see how it was going to burn. We took a rag and stick, made a torch and soaked it in the mixture, lit the torch and threw it on the soaked brush. The fire started slowly but eventually started to burn the soaked area. It burned a bit faster than diesel fuel alone, and it definitely was easier to start on fire. The sergeants thought that the burn rate was way too slow so one of the other sergeants grabbed a couple guys and went back to the POL.

This time the amount of mixed fuel that we had removed from the drum for the first burn was replaced with Mogas; now we had a much faster burning brew. We were all determined to finish our detail by noon since we now knew what we were doing. All of us were hustling. We were pouring, spraying and running. In the next hour or so we had all 55 gallons of the rapid fire tonic on about 175 or 200 yards of bunker line. We even sprayed a liquid fuel path between the areas of brush so that it would spread the flames between the vegetation patches and we wouldn't have to start them all separately. We then got a torch ready and threw it on our liquid trail.

WHAM! It didn't explode, but it did burn and spread a lot more rapidly. Instead of 15 or 20 seconds to spread down the line, it took only about eight seconds for all 200 yards to be fully inflamed. At this point we knew we had to move the truck quickly so the tires and paint wouldn't melt; it was definitely a different fire than the first one. This section of bunker line was deserted but we knew the black smoke would catch somebody's notice. So we all jumped in the trunk and went to the end, where it was much cooler for us, and waited in a somewhat inconspicuous place.

Sure enough, within in a few minutes various vehicles came to check out the smoke (and fire). Thankfully the flames from the fuel were down a bit, and by now most of the flames were from the brush. So we wandered out from the bunkers and told them about our detail and everything was cool. We didn't bother to tell them that we used more than 40% Mogas. They left, and we watched the fire burn out and were done with our detail by noon.

I think we all ate at a different unit's mess halls or were given C rations. All I remember is that we did not go back to our battalion's area because we certainly did not want them to know that we were done with our detail already. We finished lunch and drove around in the deuce and a half until 4:30 or so and turned it back in the motor pool.

We short timers were not told where to sack out with these new arrangements, but we all agreed that we were not going to point that fact out to them. We all broke up and started looking around for some abandoned buildings to sleep in. Dau Tieng was an old basecamp, and there were scores of deserted 20' x 20' tents, some with cots. Rich and I decided to find one in the general area of A Company's HQ so that we could be near our clerk. He would give us our mail and other communications and let us know if anything bad was in the air. We were far enough away from the company area to not be seen by any of our lifers. Most or all of the other short timers made similar arrangements.

The next morning, we all showed up at the battalion's roll call. The morning roll call was a morning army event where all of the enlisted men that worked at the battalion headquarters got into a formation in groups according to their jobs. So all of the cooks were in one line, the men assigned to the motor pool were in another line, all of the clerks were in another line and so on. As the Battalion Sergeant-Major (head battalion enlisted lifer) called off each section, the first man in line, usually a sergeant, would yell back, "all present and accounted for," or some other appropriate response.

The entire formation was probably 50 to 75 men, and as we approached the end of the ceremony, we were getting a bit antsy. "DIS-MISSED," was shouted and roll call was over and amazingly not one of our names had been called. All of us short timers knew instinctively to just blend into the flowing crowd and get the hell out of the area. Within five minutes, we were all together away from the battalion area, and we were stunned. They had misplaced the list of the short timer mortar men. Nobody was in charge of us, and we had just slipped between the cracks! The next morning, we got in formation again and made sure that we were in the back line because we didn't want anyone behind us to notice that we didn't report our status. When roll call finished, again there had been no call for any of us. The next day we were all hidden close enough to the formation to hear the sounds but were not actually in the formation and again there was no call for us. That was it—we were officially lost!!!

Lovejoy is walking into our hooch during our "lost weeks." When Rich and I were in Di An clearing Division, it was reported to us that the hooch had a direct mortar hit on it the night after we left.

Rich and I found a nice small hooch (made of recycled army castaway material), about 12' x 12', near the weird above-ground swimming pool and the old A Company mortar area. We soon became regulars at a nearby 155mm artillery club (a small tent that served soda and beer to their off duty artillery men). Someone in their unit had been sent the newest Beatles' album, *Abbey Road*, and for my last two weeks as a proud "Black Scarf," I just got drunk and high listening to "Here Comes the Sun," "Maxwell's Silver Hammer" and all of the rest of that great album.

It was mid-November, and Rich and I were counting down our days. Our great company clerk came over to our hideaway and offered Rich a last minute extra R and R to Hong Kong that he had somehow managed to grab. Just like my three-day pass, somehow he had snatched this R and R and sent Rich off to Hong Kong. He had obtained the signature of the CO, XO or First Sergeant, who did not notice that Rich's name on the paper appeared out of thin air. Rich just got his orders to Hong Kong, and he got the hell out of there. We didn't see him for eight days, and when he got back, Rich and I had only two or three days until we cleared Battalion. We did nothing for the next two days but clean our M16s and magazines. We were not going to slow down our trip home because some asshole said we had a dirty weapon.

PART 8

GOING HOME

CHAPTER 49

WE CLEAR BATTALION, DIVISION AND COUNTRY

Unbelievably, the day arrived to start going home! Late in the afternoon, Rich and I went over to see our company clerk at Company Headquarters. He had the papers for us to clear our company. We grabbed our papers, wished him our very best, turned in our weapons, and for the first time in a few weeks, we went to our battalion mess hall for supper. During our "Lost Period," none of us lost short-timers dared to eat at our own mess hall since someone might see us and recall that we were "lost."

We just hung out, waiting to unite with Mike and Jim. They arrived separately, and we ate and planned to meet the next day to clear Battalion together. We had all made it. As unlikely as it had seemed at certain moments, WE HAD ALL MADE IT!!! That night and the next morning it seemed so strange not to have our M16s close by or in our hands.

The next day was Thanksgiving Day. It was a Thursday, so it was business as usual. We all bounced around the different battalion buildings and departments doing various administrative clearing activities and were done by mid-afternoon. At some point, Rich and I were issued new uniforms with our names, division patches, regiment patches (we had never had one of those before), CIB and US army patches. Rich and I had spent our entire year's tour and had never had a uniform that

WE HAD ALL MADE IT!!!

had been correct and complete. This was also true for Mike. However, when Jim had been assigned his rear job he was the battalion CO's driver and had been required to look "civilized." He was expected to wear real, official uniforms with all of the correct patches and all things pretty.

We were OFF-LINE! Even though we were assigned to the 1st Infantry Division, we were not assigned to a combat unit; we all were officially OFF-LINE!!! I can't imagine that we didn't go to a club somewhere for a beer, but I actually don't remember that we did. We then went to the battalion mess hall, and I remember so well the incredible feast that was laid out for the troops. Evidently the rear echelon, with whom we were now located, celebrated the major holidays in grand fashion. The abundance of food was stunning to me. There were scores of turkey rolls, with half a dozen beautifully roasted turkeys for decoration, every side dish imaginable and two or three types of desserts. The cooks just piled the food on the trays. I just couldn't believe my eyes.

I didn't come close to finishing the fabulous food on my tray and walked outside to the tray washing station. The station was a large, screened-in room where a small army of local Vietnamese would scrape the food off the trays into large garbage drums and then wash and sanitize the metal trays. Today I can still clearly feel the disgrace I felt as I saw all of that food in the garbage and the guilt I had knowing what food my brothers in A Company would be having in the field.

I have no other memories of that day. I remember the four of us on the Dau Tieng tarmac the next day, waiting for a damned Caribou to fly us and others to Di On to clear Division. For the next two days, each of us bounced around a bigger maze of buildings and offices. We had been given a checklist of five or six places to which to report in order to collect the various parts of our master file (DA 201). So off I went on my expedition to get out of the Big Red One. I went to medical, and then finance, then personnel and so on until I had possession of my entire DA 201 file. At each stop, the clerk would initial the checklist, and I would travel to another office.

It was at some point that we found Mike's good friend Ralph O'Toole. He too was from Carroll, IA, but he also knew Jim Grey because they all went through Basic and AIT together. Ralph went over to Nam with Mike and Jim but was assigned to a different Battalion (1/18) in the 1st Division. He was also in the 1st Brigade, so we were always within thirty or forty miles from each other and many times closer. So now there were five of us processing our way home together.

The night between our two days of clearing Division all of us went to a large EM Club (Enlisted Men Club) which was a very large GI nightclub. They had a decent band made up of Koreans or Taiwanese playing American Rock and Roll. It sounded great to us, and I imagine we drank our fill of beer. We left there and flopped into our beds (we were now living in rear echelon territory so we slept in beds) and fell asleep with thoughts of home. The next morning we got up, had a fabulous breakfast and jumped into the lines at the remaining offices we needed to visit in order to finish clearing Division. The final stop was to see a recruiter for an initial on the checklist. I skipped that stop since I wasn't going to insult myself by wasting my time speaking to a recruiter. I had been forced into military life and I wasn't about to extend the hell any longer.

After the list was completed, we reported to a separate and special bunkroom from where we would catch a bus to Tan Son Nhut Air Force Base near Saigon to fly home. This was it, the last night in-country! I walked into the bunkhouse and handed the PFC clerk my checklist so that he could give me my sheets for my bed. He told me that he couldn't give the sheets for my bed to me since my list was not complete without the initials from the recruiter. I instantly became a body of molten, raging emotions inside. I looked into his eyes and very quietly told him that he was a reviled REMF (Rear Echelon Mother Fucker) and that if he didn't give me those sheets immediately that I would rip off his face with my bare hands or something to that effect. Although he knew I meant every word of the threat, he merely took a pencil, initialed the checklist and slid me my sheets. It took everything I had not to let him see me laugh at his reaction. That poor bastard had real threats to his person more than a hundred times a week and thought nothing of mine.

The next day's timeline is very foggy to me. I only remember that it was during daylight and that an army-green school bus (I think it was an Air Force bus) picked us up from the barracks and then drove us straight to Tan Son Nhut Air Force Base. It was during this trip that I allowed myself to BEGIN to think about going home. I had intellectually known that I had reached certain important milestones (like clearing Battalion and Division), but I had not allowed myself to react emotionally to them. I had seen the cruelty of fate too many times to allow me to think too far ahead.

One story will illustrate the reason I was so cautious with my feelings. When I had been an assistant gunner on what was to become my M60, my gunner was a guy named Manning. He was a patient and good teacher to me. He eventually was rewarded for his reliable service as a machine gunner by being assigned to a truck driving job in Battalion. He had finished his tour and had cleared Battalion when he was killed in the doorway of a bunker the night before he flew to Di An to clear Division. There had been some incoming an hour before and so he just stayed in the bunker for the night. No one else did, but he was a superstitious infantry short-timer. He was found in the doorway of the bunker with a cigarette between his fingers, dead from shrapnel wounds of yet another incoming set. If he had been inside the bunker (two steps), he would have been unharmed, but he had stepped out to have a cigarette.

At Tan Son Nhut, there was a respectable-looking terminal where we did a minimum of processing. The only noteworthy event was that I was called out of the line by an MP and given an extra DA 201 master file of some soldier on board who had a bad record in Nam; apparently he was not trusted to carry his own file to the states. I was told that there would be an MP at the gate in California looking for me and that I was to turn it over to him. I had been chosen because I was a sergeant. No sweat!

Next I remember walking to the plane in a quiet file of men heading home. I recalled my thoughts a year earlier when I had seen a file of men walking to their "freedom bird" and had wondered what those men were thinking. Now here I was walking to my "bird." I tried to assess my own thoughts only to discover that there was a jumble of activity in my mind. I couldn't distinguish any coherent reflections or ideas. Soon that would change, but during the moments of walking to the plane, I think that I realized that the "one year combat in hell self" stood apart from the "real world self" of the other twenty one years of my life. I think that I just couldn't get any coherent thoughts together at that point. It was as if I was sleep-walking towards the plane.

I went up the steps and found a seat, buckled in and remained in my daze. I remember thinking that only incoming mortar fire or rockets could get us now, and I knew that that was very, very unlikely. We pulled away from the terminal, taxied to the runway, and the pilot of our chartered commercial 707 pushed the throttles full forward. We were gaining speed as we thumped down the runway, and I can remember feeling the nose wheels lift as we started to rotate and prepare to launch ourselves home. But it was when the main landing gear left the runway that I knew I was going home! It was at that moment that I knew I had survived my year in hell! It was at that moment that I let my emotions go and realized that my two worlds had just been torn apart. I will never forget THAT moment!

Years later, I asked Mike Humlicek at what point he had felt that he had actually left Vietnam. He told me that when he had watched his second boot leave the tarmac and join his body on the stairway he knew he had survived. He told me that he would never forget THAT moment!

CHAPTER 50

BACK ON THE BLOCK

"We are not youth any longer. We don't want to take the world by storm. We are fleeing. We fly from ourselves. From our life. We were eighteen and had begun to love life and the world; and we had to shoot it to pieces."
—Erich Maria Remarque, *All Quiet on the Western Front*

I remember very little about the flight back home. I think we flew to Okinawa for our first refueling. It was there that I bought Mom a dinner ring. We next had another refueling stop but didn't even disembark. We then landed in Hawaii, and we walked around the terminal for forty minutes while they refueled the plane. I don't think I slept much during any part of the flights. I know I didn't on the last leg. The final stop was Travis Air Force Base, California, USA.

We landed and I thought, "I'm back on the block!" That's all we used to talk about—getting back on the block. We were greeted by another green school bus. It was here that an MP was waiting for me, and I handed over the naughty soldier's DA 201 to him. We did minimal processing at Travis and caught yet another school bus to the infamous "barn" Although I don't remember doing anything or talking much with Mike, Jim, Rich and O'Toole on the plane, we gathered back as a pack between our various rounds of processing in the barn. Those four were processing for another assignment in the States for their remaining six months in the army. I was being processed for discharge because I had wasted enough time at Ft. Wolters and on leave before Nam to have less than 5 months remaining on my two-year commitment. The policy in 1969 was to discharge and not reassign anyone returning from overseas with less than five months.

One part of the processing that was appreciated by the men who had been overseas was the steak dinner offered 24/7. There was a small mess hall that served a steak dinner any time that a person could fit it between processing duties. At some point, we all met, knowing we all had time for the dinner before any one of us would be called for our next segment of processing. It was a great meal!

In another part of the processing, each soldier was issued a new Class A (dress) uniform. It was a requirement to wear our Class A uniforms during travel. So we slowly walked through the different tailoring stations to get this done. We were measured and then handed a jacket. We later handed the jacket to another person who looked into our 201 file to see what hardware and ribbons should be put on the uniform, and then we walked on. Later we had our waists measured and then were handed pants that had trouser legs a foot too long to put on. We then walked up a small set of carpeted steps to a platform with a steel bar that looked like a yard stick vertically attached to the platform. The platform was about two and a half to three feet off the floor. Next to it was a person sitting in a chair with a piece of chalk. As we paused on the top platform the person would make a chalk mark on our pants using the top of the steel bar as the reference from the floor. From this point, which was mid-thigh, the tailors would measure down a fixed distance and sew in our nice standardized uniform cuffs.

To all of our tastes, the 1969 army's ideas of fashion were as old fashioned as its opinions on every other part of our lives. We preferred a much higher cuff than the army's rule. Everyone I knew just sleepwalked through this small fragment of our processing, and therefore all were destined to have an army uniform with the ugly army cuff length. But not Ralph O'Toole! Ralph was determined to have the only modern-looking uniform tailored that day.

As he walked up that small flight of steps to be marked for his cuff, his mind somehow emerged from its sleepless stupor, and he realized the significance of the chalk mark. He wanted high, fashionable cuffs on his pants, so as he paused and, a split-second before the chalk swipe was made, he pulled the waist of his pants so far up that he brought tears to his eyes. That chalk mark was at least 4" below anyone else's. Because he had thought to adjust his pants, he walked away feeling very, very smug. He handed in his pants and went on with his processing.

We were now getting close to the end. It was early morning on the 5th of December, the magic day for all of us. December 4th had come fast for us because we had skipped a day when we crossed the international dateline as we had flown east 24 hours getting to the States. The four of us had arrived back in the barn with our new uniforms and our big fat DA 201 files. It was at this meeting that we had a great laugh as Ralph O'Toole walked in with his new Class A uniform. We saw him from across the room with a black cloud over his head, muttering curses and growls. He cussed and growled all the way across the building to our staked-out area with our temporary bunks and duffle bags. Ralph's cuffs covered his shoes almost entirely. Of course, when Ralph's pants were being measured, he should have pushed his pants down as far as he could to get those high cuffs. We couldn't stop laughing at his comical costume, and it seemed to us that somehow our laughter was fueling the cursing.

As we looked at each other, we were greatly surprised at our uniforms. I cannot remember about O'Toole's awards, but the four of us had many more awards than we had when we shipped over to Nam in our Class A uniforms. We hadn't even known about more than half of them. Of course Jim and Rich knew about their Purple Hearts, but they had never seen them. We each had our CIBs (Combat Infantry Badges). Each of us had been awarded an Air Medal, but I don't think that we knew about them. It was given for having participated in at least twenty five helicopter combat insertions into the field. We all had been told at various times while we were on-line that we had been awarded a Bronze Star for Valor but had never seen the award or the orders. To the surprise of all of us, we had all been awarded a second Bronze Star as we left the Battalion. There were also Unit citations for being a member of the 1st Infantry Division in a combat theater. As we had stopped to pick up and change into our new Class A uniforms, we were also handed the boxes that came with the awards, along with copies of the orders for the awards. We soon stowed those away in our duffle bags or in our DA 201 files.

We were all in the barn just waiting for our names to be called for the final act of clearing. For the others, it was to get paid and receive orders for a stateside assignment; for me it was to receive my final military payment and my discharge. At some point, we determined that we all would be finished processing at about the same time very early in the morning on the 5th, so we vowed to wait until all of us were finished. We would then take a cab to San Francisco Airport together and say our goodbyes at the airport.

My name was finally called and I started towards the corridor that would take me out of the Army. For an entire year, every time we met any group of soldiers someone would yell "short," and the ritual would require every person to shout the number of months that they had left in their Vietnam tour. If a person had fewer than 90 days, then they would shout "shorter," and the ritual required replies in weeks or days. This Army sacrament was always respected, and it always produced a very pretentious winner. To soldiers with more than 6 months, the procedure was hated. When a soldier had less than 6 months, it was tolerated; with less than 3 months, it was starting to be fun; and when a person had fewer than 30 days, there were few times when he was not a winner.

This important ritual was on my mind as I approached the line for my final payday. When I got paid, I would be out of the army. As far as I knew, the Oakland Center was the only 24/7 military processing center, and since it was 1:00 a.m., I calculated that when the person in front of me was paid and out of the military that that would make me THE SHORTEST PERSON IN THE UNITED STATES ARMY. No one could claim to be shorter than me.

"Next," the clerk said. There was only one moment in my entire life that I didn't want out of the army, and this was that moment. It was *almost* a better feeling being the shortest sucker in the army than being out of the army! But that moment of weakness passed instantly; I was paid AND I WAS OUT!

I went back to the barn, and soon we were all finished. Wow! We caught a cab and headed for San Francisco Airport to catch our flights home. We arrived between 2:00 and 2:30 a.m., and the terminal was uninhabited except for a few scattered soldiers. We slowly walked and talked, checking the first flights out for each of our destinations. We just quietly talked about home. Mike, Jim and Ralph were flying to Omaha, Rich was going to Minneapolis and I was going to Washington D.C. to visit my brother Dave, who was heading for Nam in two weeks. We were quietly walking the halls like silent sharks, afraid to stop.

At some point, I happened to look behind us, and with the light just right, I noticed that at 4:30 or so the beautifully clean floors of the main terminal had a very fine layer of dust. I never would have noticed it but for the four very fine sets of footprints from our shoes and the much more noticeable 6" wide clean swaths created by O'Toole shuffling his cuffs across the clean floor. When I turned and pointed this out to our pack, a new round of howling and growling took place. We were all so very light in spirit.

Soon 5:30 rolled up to our little group, and we split up to buy our tickets home. We met back together one last time to say goodbye before we went to our different gates. I can't remember the actual scene, but I recall the incredible sensations of saying goodbye to the most important men of my life at that moment. In my immediate past life that I had shared with Mike, Jim and Rich, there had been great measures of love, fear, hope, trust, humor and staggering tragedy in the context of a brutal yet simple life. When we said goodbye, I knew that I would never live in their lives again. This is the stuff of life that makes combat veterans say that it was one of the best times of their lives. It is a brotherhood that is unlike any other bond.

My plane for D.C. left around 6:30 a.m., and I remember sitting in an aisle seat with an attractive woman seated next to me. I remember the plane being in line at the end of the runway, just minutes from takeoff. I checked to see that the stewardesses were buckled in because I wanted to lean my seat back to listen to a beautiful song. I had on those early style headphones that fit tightly in the ear canals and were very uncomfortable or even painful. I was listening as we started down the runway under full power, and I remember the takeoff.

The next thing I remember was someone shaking me awake, telling me to bring my seat upright for landing preparations for our Dulles Airport landing. I had slept through two meals, three time zones and all of the five-hour flight. I probably had produced a pool of drool the size of my entire uniform front. I woke up to an excruciating pain caused by those shitty airline headphones. I was now fully awake, and within minutes I would be seeing my family.

We off-loaded onto those weird Dulles Airport buses and headed for the terminal. As I entered the terminal, I was scanning the crowd for Mom and my brother Dave since I knew they would be meeting me there. I spotted Dave first, and he pointed to Mom who was looking in a slightly different direction. Dave had told her that he thought that he had spotted me in another direction and got her looking at a different crowd. This allowed me to walk right up to her and then surprise her with and a hug and a kiss. We wept tears of joy. Thanks, Dave.

I cannot imagine her emotions at having me return safely. Her fiancé/husband had been drafted into the army six months before World War II and not discharged until six months *after* the war ended. She was a recent widow, she was having another son go over to the war zone in two weeks and she had three more kids in school at home. That's a full plate, but she knew that a person should celebrate one win at a time, and our hug was a great victory.

We loaded ourselves and my one duffle bag into the car and drove to Dave's home in Virginia. Dave's wife Cheryl had returned from work and was cooking a celebratory meal. We all had a great time eating, drinking, laughing and teasing, and then I collapsed. I said goodnight and went to my room. Out of necessity, for a year I had stopped thinking about anything other than getting home, and here I was. I slipped between clean sheets and reveled at the thought of my only dream coming true. I was home, I was with my family and I was unhurt. I fell asleep immediately, flooded with joy.

PART 9

EMERGING FROM THE BLACK MENTAL FOG

"We don't receive wisdom; we must discover it for ourselves after a journey that no one can take for us or spare us."
—Marcel Proust

Overview

After returning home from Vietnam, I lived in a black mental fog. I always assumed this toxic brew of unstable emotions was a direct result of my combat experiences. However, over time I have come to realize that this toxic brew was comprised of more than just the experiences of combat; swirling around in my mind were also the issues related to the human environment of war and my personal adjustments and reactions to all of it. As I wrap up this book, I have become aware of the surprising, and to me, remarkable way I am processing these events now. With some research and a lot of hard work I seem to have been able to separate the black mental fog into several matters that I have had to deal with since my return to "The World." In the following chapters, I discuss the insights that I have gained over the years and during the process of writing this book.

CHAPTER 51

DEMONS AND GHOSTS

"Full moon is falling through the sky.
Cranes fly through clouds.
Wolves howl. I cannot find rest
Because I am powerless
To amend a broken world."
—Guy Gavriel Kay, *Under Heaven*

My war experiences generated a multitude of demons and ghosts that have haunted me since returning home. At first, I worked hard and drank hard. The alcohol seemed to numb the memories and feelings somewhat, and that was enough for a while. Eventually, the desire to return to a more normal life took over, so I sobered up and started setting goals, including those of completing school and finding more meaningful work. Around the same time, I met Penny and fell in love. We were married; I finished college and found meaningful work. In many ways, my life was normal, but I still lived with the residue of wartime demons in my life.

For the next forty years, I continued to wrestle with these demons intermittently. I again struggled with them through the process of writing this manuscript. For me, the haunts concerned two major questions: "How did I come to the point that I could kill a human being?" and "Why did I survive when so many other good men did not?" In this chapter I deal with the first question.

Our wedding day in a 150 year old country wedding chapel

First, without a doubt, learning to kill and act inhumanly is a huge adjustment for most nineteen and twenty year olds. There has always been and will always be an enormous lifelong change in each of those young persons. This usually leads to one inescapable hurdle that must be addressed at some point—the moral justification of one's personal acts of war.

I have come to the conclusion that morality is a large can of worms. It is an ethnic, tribal, religious and/or national tool for modifying behavior and for justifying some distasteful event or policy. Our leaders, whether national, political or religious, demonize our/their antagonists in order to elicit emotional responses rather than encourage rational debate when discussing a moral question. This demonizing is used as a shortcut around reasonable debate in order to swiftly persuade us to agree with their ultimate goal—whether it involves supporting the moral status quo or changing it. I see the application of this practice today on both sides of the abortion discussion, the gay rights debate and the death penalty question as well as many more issues.

So if morality itself is a quagmire of competing and unsettled ideas of behavior and thinking, then how does anyone try to justify any action? Killing people and causing misery are the deeds of war and usually need to be morally reckoned. As I came to face these questions over time and had to weigh my actions, I knew I had to consider both the context of the acts and my moral values *at the time* of my deeds in order to fully and fairly deal with my moral questioning.

I read somewhere to never forget that the root of the French term infantry is *infant.* Youthful recruits are still forming their morality and usually are molded more effectively into soldiers to do society's dirty work than older soldiers. In our training, we and the enemy were dehumanized to a point where many of us might well have lost some of our humanity and morality. So for me when I got to the time when I knew I had to face this can of worms, several questions formed in my mind. First, was I strong enough in my beliefs to resist the army's view of morality? After all, I had never been tested before so I never had to even question what I thought was my moral conduct. A better question might be the following—what was my moral foundation when I went into the army?

Growing up, I think I had absorbed both an American-Post-World-War-II-military-service ethic and a Judeo-Christian "Thou shall not kill" ethic. Steeped in the ignorance of what war was really like, I think I gave in to the more effective, or perhaps the word is more powerful, societal pressure to serve in the military. I don't remember very much moral church pressure to counter the "we'll throw you in prison" position of the government. So I guess I bowed to the much more clearly stated societal pressure and went into the military.

Once I got over to Nam, the whole question of "why am I here?" was moot. My moral behavior had to be considered in the context of the place and time in which I found myself and that demanded a whole different moral dialogue. In my case, the assignment was to kill as many people as I could within my mission parameters. Those restrictions were usually obvious when we were hunting on the Ho Chi Minh Trail, soldier against soldier in a shootout. To me it was a much easier moral task to defend those actions. I started with the fact that I wanted to survive my tour and that I would probably kill people to get home. But then there were these pertinent questions—"are there any moral limits to the act of killing in a war zone," and "if there are limits, what are they?"

As to the first question, I knew my answer was yes; there were limits. Killing and maiming anybody and everybody to get home could never even be thought of as a possibility. So then I had to determine what the limits were. I believe only persons who were a direct threat to me were legally and morally my enemies. Further, I believe there must be no "pay backs" or "frustration kills" or "rage kills" allowed. Paybacks, frustration and rage may be used as explanations or rationales, or may even sound like appropriate responses, but to me, these responses were and are totally unacceptable. But I was also very fortunate that I wasn't in a combat situation that had daily hard-fought fights for months at a time like some soldiers in World War II. I simply don't know if I could have stood the pain of the losses. So what is my limit? To quote The Humanity Healing Network (2009), I had to preserve my "resilience to keep [my] humanity in the face of inhumanity."

After many years of thought, I have come to the conclusion that I never did more than was necessary to get home. Even though I sometimes find it difficult to justify my being in Vietnam, I do know that I never, or, to my knowledge, my platoon or company never participated in any action that I thought went beyond a legal and moral mission. That is not to say that there were times when other units broke down or were ordered to engage in actions beyond these moral limits. In fact there is a growing body of information being brought out recently about commanders ordering such actions. But as far as I know, Alpha Company's men never did. This realization has done a lot towards slaying some of my demons.

The other part that's hard to justify is this: when I was 20 years old, why was I so naïve about the life and death choices that all males my age were being forced to make at the time? I really never had an inner dialogue about whether to let myself be swept into the war or to choose to go to Canada to avoid the war. I chose to ignore the world and make no decision. As always, not to choose is a choice. This one still haunts me.

Once we got on-line, the only focus one could have was to do what it took to get through the hell; morally a soldier should do no more. Going beyond what is necessary to accomplish the mission (such as taking additional action out of anger or revenge) can lead a soldier to challenge his morality. For much of the first two and a half years that I was home, I was drunk most of the time that I wasn't working. The drunken numbness allowed me to put some distance (time) between me and my ghosts and allowed me a bit of slack with my adjustment to civilian life. The more philosophical process began in earnest shortly after I decided to quit drinking excessively and to rejoin the world. When one shifts the moral basis of one's life back and forth, it takes a toll, and the adjustments that are made are often not clean or pleasant.

CHAPTER 52

THE GUILT OF SURVIVAL

The second source of my turmoil has been my "guilt of survival." Why did I survive when so many other good men did not?

When I am alone for a couple of days, it is not unusual for my thoughts to return to my time in Vietnam, and I often wrestle with my guilt of surviving the year. My soul needs an ongoing accounting of that extremely tricky matter. The problem is that it is very difficult to come up with anything other than my flippant "life is a crapshoot." At times that explains a great deal, but it seems like there has to be a better answer.

Life on-line was extremely boring or extremely loud, smoky, smelly, hot, fast, illogical, dangerous, indiscriminate and random. It didn't take long on-line to realize that life was truly a crapshoot. We all lived with certain knowledge that we needed both skill and luck to get home because there were too many times when the person right next to you got killed and you didn't.

But here's the rub—those unfortunate men were most often good, fun, sincere husbands and sons who deserved a better fate than the one they got, especially "compared to me with all my faults."

"I was just standing there," or "I am normally in that position," or "why was I called over to . . .?" are the thoughts that all of us survivors have, over and over and over, thoughts that remain stuck in the same faulty groove on our mental CDs.

Every single random act can and will be overanalyzed. That's why it never goes away. "Someone should have stopped Petey from crawling out into that Hell."

Of course there is another way to view it—that cosmically we are all fly specks, and it really didn't matter whether any one of us made it home or not. Typically I am very good at not assuming guilt in my life. However, this is one type of guilt I just cannot shake. I saw too many good men die or become monsters. My take is that if there is a meaning to life, one must assume this survivor's guilt and wear it because if there is no meaning, then it doesn't really matter if one survives a war or not.

CHAPTER 53

NOTHING BUT A FAILURE OF LEADERSHIP

War is a racket.
—Major General Smedley Butler, USMC,
War Is a Racket

As I was thinking about my military life and jotting down notes for this piece, I discovered that I didn't recall memories of us doing rational mission-oriented exercises as much as I recalled the missions that were promotion-oriented for the lifers. The many worthless lifers weren't trying to wage war to win; they were making opportunities for themselves to get promotions. From my perspective, the individual draft infantry soldier fought effectively in spite of our senior leadership. I say "in spite of" because most infantry lifers were just horsing around with the game pieces and getting in a couple of tours so that they could advance up the ladder. They all knew there wouldn't be fast and easy promotions and awards after the war. My anger is not aimed at the few good infantry lifers or the many career personnel that supplied me or supported me; rather, it is reserved for the *infantry leadership* who failed to see and/or stop the heavy casualties caused by the eager, promotion-hungry lifer corps. These lifers would have let the war and their selfish acts go on forever. With all of this incompetence, we grunts were as powerless in the field as I was on the four inch dot my first day at Ft. Polk.

As to the question of whether this lethal situation existed due to a flawed system or flawed individuals, the answer makes little difference to me. There were scores of poorly-conceived and reckless missions and field decisions in my company and higher that put the unlimited draftee infantrymen at high risk, and that produced few results and many needless casualties. Our leadership created an environment that hatched idiotic missions with dubious results. If the missions succeeded, then there would be feathers in their caps; if the missions failed or sustained heavy casualties, there would be no consequences. There were never any consequences for casualties in my outfit. Most of our leaders were absolute failures!

CHAPTER 54

MY DEEP-SEATED ANGER

I now understand that my gift from these lifers was a hair-trigger rage that lies just below the surface of my daily life and that had its beginning as frustration and powerlessness against their self-centeredness. When I came home, I was happy to have survived my combat tour. I started my new life with two consequences of my tour. First, in spite of my tour and the resulting fatalism, I was able to restart living my life with an optimistic attitude; after all, I thought, if I can get through that year, I can get through anything. Secondly, I came home with a lingering fury.

Fortunately, my everyday personality is ruled by the first consequence, and I am considered to be a functioning, easy-going person to many. Unfortunately, to the love of my life, I can be very difficult. At times I have very little patience with Penny and will fly off the handle with her. During those times, she needs to be constantly on edge because she is afraid that I will yell or criticize her very loudly. The irony is that the one person with whom I can be the most at ease is the person that feels my fury the most. At times I deny that I have the problem of a hair-trigger rage; at other times I admit to it, but I have been reluctant go to private therapy for it. I have always known that it was caused by the army, and I have wanted them to be accountable. Since 1970, I have made a number of attempts to be diagnosed or treated for Post-Traumatic Stress Disorder with the VA, but they have never given me an appointment to be screened for it. By 1980, I gave up on the God Damned Iowa VA system.

In January of 2011, Penny and I moved to Arkansas for our retirement. I was encouraged by many friends to try the Arkansas VA system. Wow, what a difference! The VA has finally taken some responsibility in dealing with some of my service-connected problems. Most importantly, after 43 years, the VA finally let me see someone to find out if I had PTSD. I have seen a Psychiatrist who diagnosed me as having PTSD; I am now in the process of working with a therapist to help me improve myself in several identified problem areas in my life. Penny tells me that life is better with me—thank God!

I am enjoying my new hearing aids from the VA and have been placed back in the Agent Orange registry. Relations seem to be better between the VA system and me now. For that I am grateful.

CHAPTER 55

EMOTIONAL NUMBNESS

The last piece I wrote for this book was the account of my Platoon Leader, Lt. Pratt's, dying, as I knelt beside him. I hadn't remembered that event until I had peeled away many layers of consciousness and other stories through the process of writing this book. My recollection of that event is causing me to examine my response to death and other emotional events in my life today. I was surprised at how cold it sounded when I read that we simply accepted the death and then, quite rationally and correctly, went back to work.

I recall a few years after I came home, Penny and I used to drive to Sac City, IA and visit her parents four to six times a year. Coincidentally two of my best friends from Vietnam, Mike Humlicek and Jim Grey, each lived within one hour's driving time from Sac City. Yet I only got together with both of them once, and I visited with Mike only one or two additional times. Until recently, I hadn't been in touch with either of them for more than 25 or 30 years.

After the army, Jim returned home, went straight back to school and completed a Master's Degree in counseling. The one time that the three of us got together, in 1990, we eventually started to talk about our lives since we returned to the States. I remember Jim saying that there was a body of research that indicated combat veterans often develop a stunted emotional range as a coping mechanism to their life in combat. They never allow themselves either great joy or sorrow, probably because it requires an emotional investment that they just can't afford to make while in combat. He thought at the time that he had continued that pattern to that day; Mike and I agreed that we too had experienced stunted emotions both in combat and after.

Several years before I started this book, I suddenly found myself tearing and quietly crying at sweet, sugar-infused TV shows and commercials. I couldn't seem to stop the waterworks. For example, I was crying watching Penny's Christmas movies on the Hallmark Channel. I'm still doing it; I have no control.

A couple of months ago, Mike Humlicek and his wife met with Penny and me for dinner and, without prompting, he told us that five years earlier he had started doing the same thing. He told us that he continues to weep today and doesn't understand it. I think that we, and many more combat veterans, are emotionally damaged. Maybe Jim was right; our extreme joyous and tragic moments have been taken from us. Maybe many, many other poignant, essential, private moments are lost to us because of our war experience. How did that affect our marriages or crucial parenting moments with our kids or our lives in general? I didn't grieve my sister's death, my father-in-law's death or celebrate my 40 year wedding anniversary fully. What other important moments have I simply failed to feel fully? How many times have I failed my family and friends with these kinds of responses or with a lack of any response?

Everybody's life falls short of their ideal. "Shut up, you whiners, and get back to living," is the call from the civilian sidelines. I agree, but don't forget, many veterans simply wish they knew how. I need to learn how to stop the uncontrolled waterworks and start to grieve and celebrate.

CHAPTER 56

UNDERSTANDING HUMANITY AND THE HUMAN EXPERIENCE

One difference in me after my 19½ months in the military was the drastic change in my understanding of humanity and the human experience. In 1968, the draft was taking everyone. I lived with a true geographic, social, cultural and economic cross section of the United States. I am very thankful for that because I experienced a far wider spectrum of fellow Americans than many people get a chance to experience. On the other hand, the spectrum that I worked and lived with included not only the kind, the passionate, the smart, the fun and the near normal; it also included the stupid, the ignorant, the naive, the passive, the aggressive, the crazy, and the truly psychopathic. On a daily basis, I had to deal with any and all of these *armed* individuals, and it was not always easy. For the remainder of my life, I interacted with few personalities or situations that I was not in most ways prepared to deal with. That diversity of people and power was a real eye opener to a naive Iowa kid.

However, I must say that I personally resent that my government made me deal and live for some months with the two soldiers in our company that were psychopathic killers. Several times my comrades and I witnessed or stopped extremely psychotic episodes with these armed men. The clearest event in memory occurred the morning after our shootout on the bunker line in Quan Loi. That next morning, one of those nuts went into the Battalion Aid Station, walked up to a bed and killed a severely wounded, bed-ridden NVA soldier captured the previous night. He then simply walked out—with absolutely no consequences. These events were known to and accepted by the army and its lifer corps. The army wanted killers and they didn't want to lose those two. The NVA were not always the ones to be feared during my tour.

CHAPTER 57

THE BONDS OF COMBAT FRIENDSHIPS

"The army might screw you and your girlfriend might dump you and the enemy might kill you, but the shared commitment to safeguard one another's lives is unnegotiable and only deepens with time."
—Sebastian Junger, *War*

I just recently returned from an army 2nd Infantry Regiment Reunion at which I spent a weekend with seven men that were in Alpha Company in the same time frame that I was in the company. We were all survivors of the particular hell that was dished up to us in heaping portions by our fate, our country and our military leadership. We are the lucky ones that are still standing. I had not been in their company for forty six years and, except for their older faces, it was like I was returning from a one week R and R

Just being in their presence humbled me.

These were the very men that guarded my back, got me out of my jams, watched over my shoulder, covered my ass and performed every other real life cliché, but these acts were for real. I relied on every one of them, every hour of every day

After being in the rarified company of my friends in Alpha Company after those many years absence, I know for certain that these friendships are the closest friendships that I have.

Because of the life and death origin of these ties, in several ways these are stronger than family bonds.

CHAPTER 58

A NEWFOUND RESPECT

Through this very difficult writing experience, I have actually changed my perspective about my life, my service and therefore myself. I have developed respect, not for any actions during my service, but rather for having survived over there and here, in having served my country honorably, in having become an effective soldier, and in having faced this writing task, doing the work to see it through and make some sense of my life. For over forty years, I had difficulty separating anything good from all of the rage and powerlessness bundled into a big black knot in my mind and soul. Absolutely nothing good came out of any part of it the whole time I ignored it. But now I have been forced to unravel the tangle and deal with every point separately, and I am a better person for it.

My view now is that however I ended up over there, I accepted the new reality and did my best to protect myself and my fellow soldiers. I respect my ability to have been able to adapt to and endure the irresponsible lifer culture that was so prevalent in our lives. I also respect my resolve to learn the whole new craft of warfare well enough to have helped myself and others get home. I now have a sense of pride in my service that I didn't have before writing this book. I never supported the Vietnam War, and I still don't, but I did heed my country's call (however misguided our leaders were), and I did sacrifice body and soul because of it. For more than forty years I have survived, where many others have not. I believe I have come to terms with my moral questions. I have accepted my guilt of survival as a permanent part of me. I am trying to learn to focus my fury at the worthless fucking lifers who were in my life. I have finally accepted my military awards as a tribute to my being a good enough soldier to help bring back home as many of my fellow grunts as I could.

The year in Vietnam was, without a doubt, the worst time in my life. But I now understand that in many ways it was also a positive time in my life. More than any other factor, that time in Nam shaped me into the adult I am today. That tour matured me and made me simplify my moral and ethical scheme right down to my essence. And it gave me a deeper understanding of the wonders of friendship and trust. I now finally have pride in both myself and my life.

. . . Yet having said all of that, forty some years later, I would give almost anything to have my body pumped full of adrenalin in anticipation, standing on the skid of a slick going into an LZ, or flying back to basecamp with my legs hanging out of the chopper door, cooling off and letting down. In the words of Charles Dickens in *A Tale of Two Cities*, "It was the best of times; it was the worst of times . . ."

GLOSSARY

50 cal - US .50 caliber heavy machine gun

51 cal - Enemy heavy machine gun

81 mm mortar - US mortar assigned to infantry companies in Vietnam

82 mm - A mortar used by the North Vietnamese Army (NVA) and Viet Cong (VC)

105 - A 105-mm howitzer, one of the smallest artillery guns used by the US Army in Vietnam. Ground troops relied heavily on 105 for close support

201 file - a US Army personnel file

Agent Orange - Widely used herbicide; a defoliant effective against broadleaf plants

Airmobile - Helicopter-borne; 1st Infantry Division was airmobile in Vietnam

AIT - Advanced Infantry Training

AK-47 - NVA and VC semi-automatic or automatic assault weapon that used 7.62mm short ammo

Ambush - Formation used to kill the enemy from cover without warning and usually set up at night

AO - Area of Operations

APC - M113 Armored Personnel Carrier

ARVN - Army of the Republic of Vietnam; South Vietnamese government forces

AWOL - Absent With Out Leave; unauthorized absence

Basecamp - Semi-permanent field headquarters; usually contains all or part of a large unit's support elements like artillery, medical and engineers units

Bde - Brigade; military organizational unit of approximately 3,000 to 5,000 soldiers

Bn - Battalion; military unit of around 500-1500 men usually consisting of between two and six companies and typically commanded by a lieutenant colonel

Bronco - OV-10 twin-engine aircraft armed with rockets and mini-guns; used as an aircraft or artillery spotter or a scout

Bush - Slang infantry term for the field

Caribou - C7 Caribou; a twin-engine light transport aircraft operated by the Air Force as a taxi in Vietnam.

Chinook - Large twin-rotor helicopter; also known as a shithook

CIB - Combat Infantry Badge. An US Army award for being under enemy fire in Vietnam for more than thirty days; worn on both fatigues and dress uniforms.

Claymore - M18A1 directional anti-personnel mine with 900 steel balls firing in a pattern like a shotgun

Click - Kilometer

Cloverleaf - Sweeps in several directions by groups of three to five men in the bush to look for and report any enemy material or activity; employed four to eight times daily during routine patrols

Cobra - AH-1 Cobra; a two-bladed attack helicopter for close ground support

Company - a military unit, typically consisting of 80–130 soldiers and usually commanded by a captain

CO - Commanding Officer

Contact - Engagement with the enemy

CP - Command Post

C130 - Troop and cargo aircraft

C4 - Type of plastic explosive; the explosive used in claymore mines

C-rations - "C"s; Combat Rations; canned meals for use in the field

CS - A riot-control gas which when used burns the eyes and mucus membranes of the soldiers

Defoliant - Chemical sprayed on trees and plants to make leaves fall off; the most commonly used defoliant in Vietnam was Agent Orange

Div - Division; a large military unit or formation, usually consisting of between 10,000 and 30,000 soldiers

Deuce-and-a-Half - Large 3-axle military truck: Two-and-a-half ton truck

Dustoff - The radio code-word for calling in a Medevac helicopter

FDC - Fire-Direction Control; a squad in a mortar platoon in which radio requests for fire support were calculated into specific information for ground artillery and mortar crews to set up their guns to fire

Firebase - A defended location in an AO from which support operations such as artillery are located; small basecamp

FNG - "Fucking New Guy"

Frag - Fragmentation hand grenade

Fragging - Assassination of unpopular lifers (career soldiers), often by means of fragmentation grenade

Free-Fire Zone - a designated area with no restrictions on the use of fire power

GI - Government Issue; slang term for all individual US military personnel

Grunt - US slang for infantry soldier

H&I - Harassment and Interdiction; random artillery, mortar or air bombardment on locations which might be or have been used by enemy forces; usually fired at night

HE - High Explosive artillery or mortar round

Hot LZ - Landing Zone under enemy fire

Hump - March or patrol in the field or to perform any grueling task

In-Country - In Vietnam

Inf - Infantry

Jungle Penetrator - Heavy egg-shaped cage with folding seats lowered from a helicopter to extract wounded soldiers in heavy foliage where a landing zone is not possible

KIA - Killed In Action

Leg - Slang term for an Army infantry soldier

Lifer - A career military man; in Vietnam the term was used in a derogatory manner

LZ - Landing Zone

MEDEVAC - Medical evacuation usually by helicopter

Medic - Soldier medically trained to provide critical initial medical treatment in the field

Mermite - Large insulated food containers used to carry hot meals to soldiers in the field

Mess/Mess Hall - Dining hall in basecamp

Mini-Gun - Small Gatling gun; 7.62mm machine gun comprising 6-10 rotating barrels capable of firing up to 6000 rounds per minute. Often mounted on airplanes and helicopters and used on ground targets

Mogas - Military gasoline

Mortar - Infantry support weapon which fires bombs in a high trajectory. In Vietnam the 81mm and the 4.2 inch mortars were used by the US Infantry

M14 - M14 rifle; a selective-fire automatic rifle that fires 7.62×51mm NATO (.308 Winchester) ammunition. Also used as a sniper rifle in Vietnam

M16 - 5.56mm lightweight personal rifle; primary infantry rifle issued in Vietnam

M60 - General purpose machine gun

M79 - 40mm grenade launcher

M113 - Armored personnel carrier designed to carry troops

Nam - Slang for Vietnam

Napalm - Mixture of gasoline and detergent used for close air support for infantry troops during firefights

NCO - Non-Commissioned Officer such as a sergeant

NDP - Night Defensive Position in the bush where infantry dug in for the night

NVA - North Vietnamese Army; regular army of North Vietnam

OCS - Officer Candidate School

On-Line - Working as an infantry unit outside an armed and defendable outpost or basecamp

P-38 - A small collapsible can opener

Patrol - Action of a collection of soldiers (from squad to company in size) to search for the enemy or information and materials of the enemy

Platoon - A military unit composed of four squads. A platoon usually consisted of fifteen to thirty soldiers

Point Squad - First men in both columns during patrols

Poncho Liner - A quilted tough nylon blanket carried for warmth in the field

Pop Ambush - To initiate an ambush by detonating the claymore mines

Pop Smoke - To throw a colored (red, yellow, or green) smoke grenade to assist helicopters in identifying correct landing place or as aids in determining the location of friendly forces and enemy targets

PRC-25 or Prick 25 - Portable Radio Communications, Model 25; the radio that the infantry carried into the field

Puff the Magic Dragon/Spooky - C-47 aircraft armed with three mini-guns that could fire 12,000 rounds per minute.

PX - Post Exchange; retail stores for military personnel; in Vietnam, located in large basecamps

Rank - Designation of authority

REMF - "Rear Echelon Mother Fucker;" infantry slang for anyone that was not an infantryman

Rome Plow - A huge bulldozer used to clear dense jungle away from roadsides to prevent close range enemy ambushes on friendly truck convoys

ROTC - Reserve Officer Training Corps is a college-based program for training commissioned officers

RPG - Rocket-Propelled Grenades; Soviet shoulder-fired rocket propelled grenade; used as assault weapons by NVA and VC

R&R - Rest and Recreation; seven-day vacation for GIs outside of South Vietnam

RTO - Radio Telephone Operator; the soldier that carried the radio on his back in the field.

Ruff Puff - A derogatory term used by GIs for Vietnamese National Police

Sapper - North Vietnamese Army (NVA) or VC soldiers who penetrated bases and carried satchels filled with explosives used to destroy infrastructure and kill soldiers

Shithook - Large twin-rotor helicopter; also known as a Chinook

Short - A soldier having less time left in-country than another soldier, as in "I'm shorter than you"

Slick - Slang for a UH-1D individual troop- and cargo-carrying helicopter

Squad - A small military unit, usually led by a non-commissioned officer (NCO), consisting of four to seven men

Spooky/Puff the Magic Dragon - C-47 aircraft armed with three mini-guns that could fire 12,000 rounds per minute.

Starlight Scope - Early night vision device that used existing light from the moon and stars to brighten targets at night; a worthless tool in the dense jungle and forested areas that had over-cover because of lack of light

Steel Pot - The standard U.S. Army helmet

Sweep - Tactical move through an area to check for bodies, intelligence, equipment, etc.

Track - slang for an M113 armored personnel carrier

Tracers - Special bullets containing phosphorous that burns brightly while in motion to display their trajectory. US forces used red and the enemy used green tracers

Viet Cong (VC) - Enemy forces belonging to the communist National Liberation Front

White Phosphorus - Explosive round fired from artillery, mortar, or rockets, which dispersed dense white smoke and was used as a spot marker by ground forces; it also caused serious burns; also known by the slang terms "Willie Peter" and "Wilson Picket"

WIA - Wounded In Action

Zippo - Cigarette lighter; also a M113 APC fitted with a flame-thrower

ABOUT THE AUTHOR

Douglas Beed was forced into the military in the spring of 1968. He eventually ended up in the U.S. Army infantry and was asked to do a variety of jobs for his company. He spent a total of nineteen and a half months and was honorably separated in December 1969 with a Combat Infantry Badge, a Bronze Star with V (valorous) Device and Oak Leaf Cluster, and an Air Medal.

He and his wife Penny are now retired and reside in central Arkansas. Retirement followed a career that included working in the construction trades, being a commercial aerial painting contractor, and teaching as a college professor in a construction management program.

His first writing project began as a collection of infantry stories originally composed at the request of his nieces and nephews.

